Gerhard Uhlhorn, Charles Edward Grinnell

The modern representations of the life of Jesus

Gerhard Uhlhorn, Charles Edward Grinnell

The modern representations of the life of Jesus

ISBN/EAN: 9783337775308

Printed in Europe, USA, Canada, Australia, Japan

Cover: Foto ©Lupo / pixelio.de

More available books at **www.hansebooks.com**

MODERN REPRESENTATIONS

OF THE

LIFE OF JESUS.

THE

MODERN REPRESENTATIONS

OF THE

LIFE OF JESUS.

FOUR DISCOURSES

DELIVERED BEFORE THE EVANGELICAL UNION AT HANOVER, GERMANY.

By Dr. GERHARD UHLHORN,

FIRST PREACHER TO THE COURT.

TRANSLATED FROM THE THIRD GERMAN EDITION,

By CHARLES E. GRINNELL.

BOSTON:
LITTLE, BROWN, AND COMPANY.
1868.

PREFACE

BY THE TRANSLATOR.

THESE excellent discourses have been translated because they present a fair, broad, and clear view of the modern controversies concerning the life of Jesus Christ, from a standpoint of supernaturalism. It is hoped that their scientific array of arguments may be of use to some who are already familiar with their substance, and that their popular form may serve to attract to divine learning some who do not know the strength of the foundations of the Christian religion.

The theology of the learned Author, so far as it is indicated by these historical discourses, differs from that of the translator; but it does not interfere with the historical purpose of the translation.

The original discourses are not furnished with references to the pages, volumes, or editions of the works of Renan, Schenkel, or Strauss, from which quotations are made. The quotations have been verified; and it is thought that the addition to the translation of definite references to the books criticised, with corresponding references to the English translations of those books, may be of service. References have also been subjoined to those quotations in the notes which the translator has been able to verify. The learned Author quotes the meaning, but not the letter, of Kepler, Ritter, and Agassiz. The substantial quotations from Kepler and Ritter are translated as given in the original Notes; but the translator has taken the liberty to substitute Agassiz's own English words in place of a translation of a paraphrase.

The editions referred to in the following pages are — "Vie de Jésus." Par Ernest Renan. Douzième édition. Boston: De Vries, Ibarra, et Cie. — "The Life of Jesus." By Ernest Renan. Translated from the original French by Charles Edwin Wilbour. New York: Carleton, 1864. — "Das Characterbild Jesu." Ein biblicher Versuch. Von Dr. Daniel Schenkel. Dritte Auflage. Wiesbaden: C. W. Kreidel's Verlag, 1864. — "The Character of Jesus Portrayed." A Biblical Essay, with an Appendix. By Dr. Daniel Schenkel. Translated from the third German edition, with Introduction and Notes, by W. H. Furness, D.D. Boston: Little,

Brown, & Co., 1866. — "Das Leben Jesu, für das deutsche Volk gearbeitet." Von David Friedrich Strauss. Zweite Auflage. Leipzig: F. A. Brockhaus, 1864. — "A New Life of Jesus." By David Friedrich Strauss. Authorized Translation, 2 vols. London and Edinburgh: Williams & Norgate, 1865.

C. E. G.

LOWELL, MASSACHUSETTS,
    May 1, 1868.

PREFACE

BY THE AUTHOR.

I HAVE determined, only after repeated requests, to publish the following discourses, which I delivered this winter before the Evangelical Union. It is with such discourses as with sermons: without attributing any special value to them, one should not withhold them from those who may wish to read them in private, or to communicate them to others. I have therefore left them, with unessential alterations, just as they were. They are meant to be the same discourses which I delivered. It did not seem to me to accord with the character of such discourses, to furnish them with citations to which I did not refer in the delivery. Since citations are often only the expression of thanks to those from whom one has learned something, these thanks may here be generally expressed. Popular discourses are not intended to impart new investigations: I wish simply to repeat to my hearers what I myself have learned from others. It seemed, however, to be well to add in the Notes several things which the limited time of delivery excluded from the discourses. The choice of these additions rests in great part upon conversations with my hearers, and their consequent requests.

May the Lord bless the printed word, as I hope He has permitted the spoken word to be not without a blessing!

Hanover, Feb. 8, 1866.

CONTENTS.

FIRST DISCOURSE.
	PAGE
THE LIFE OF JESUS BY RENAN	1

SECOND DISCOURSE.
"THE CHARACTER OF JESUS PORTRAYED," BY SCHENKEL; "A NEW LIFE OF JESUS," BY STRAUSS . . 34

THIRD DISCOURSE.
THE GOSPELS 78

FOURTH DISCOURSE.
THE MIRACLES 116

FIRST DISCOURSE.

THE LIFE OF JESUS BY RENAN.

SINCE the first days of the Church, when she had to defend her faith against heathen calumny and heathen science, the attacks upon Christianity and the Church have never been so manifold and so powerful as at the present time. The contest is no longer upon single questions, such as whether this or that conception of Christianity is the more correct; but the very existence of Christianity is at stake. Though the final goal, the destruction of Christianity and the Church, is concealed in many of these assaults; though they pretend to undertake to lead back Christian faith and life to its original purity and simplicity, — but little acuteness is needed to perceive, that this is mere show, — that they really attempt to set aside that at least which has been known up to this time as Christianity. But, thank God, there is also no lack of defenders of the invaded sanctuary; and it can also be truly said, that at no time has the apologetical activity in the Church been so lively as at present. A whole literature of this tenor has grown up of late years; and in most of the larger cities of our Fatherland, during this time, apologetical discourses have been orally delivered, certainly not without a blessing.

It is true, one must avoid overvaluing such attempts at defence. The best defence is, and must always remain, the simple, faithful preaching of the gospel, and the real witness of the power of Christianity in life and conversation. The most correct course of defence is found upon the first page of the Gospel, where Philip answers to the doubt of Nathanael, " Come and see." But, even if Christianity can be demonstrated to nobody, he who has seen and experienced nothing of it can take nothing from it. In spite of all that, however, apologetical activity has in all cases great importance.

The circle in which books are read which have undertaken to attack Christianity, is comparatively small. No German work has had a circulation approaching that of Renan's book in France; and how many have the time and desire to read through such comprehensive writings as those of Strauss and Schenkel? How many there are who content themselves with the knowledge of having it down in black and white, that it is all over with Christianity! But the circle is considerably greater in which those writings have at least an indirect influence. This influence is exerted through the periodical press. The daily and weekly newspapers, and the monthly magazines, take up the matter as one adapted to the times, and communicate, in a brief and popular way, to the greater public the pretended results of those writings. Hence arises a kind of public opinion upon the subject; and an uncertainty, at least, widely prevails whether the foundations of Christianity are sound,—an uncertainty which, from being more dangerous the less able one is to investigate the questions, hinders many from coming to Christianity. Now, as has been already said, although we may be unable to demonstrate Christianity to any one, we can nevertheless remove such hindrances; and it is our duty to do so.

From the pulpit this is a difficult, if not an impossible, task; for the service of public worship is an occasion for building up the people in their faith, and not for proving this faith in the first place. Here the sermon itself must be prepared beforehand, since the preacher in writing and in speaking avoids general controversy, and declares the sound — yes, the scientifically and historically sound — confirmation of the Christian faith. In writing and speaking, I say; for just here the living word has great importance. As a sermon which is printed and read is never so effective as one which is spoken and heard, even if the latter is inferior to the former in many points of matter and style, so it is with essays of this kind. There is always something dead in the letter, and it can never fill the place of the living person. I would earnestly entreat you to give the benefit of this remark to me. I do not pretend to be able to give you much that is new, which may not have been already said elsewhere, and better than I can say it; but I do not believe that it is therefore sufficient to merely refer you to printed essays and books upon the subject. I think that the living word, even when it does not comprehend so much, may be worth hearing.

The attacks upon the Christian faith, different as they are, have essentially one aim,—which is, to set aside the supernatural in Christianity, and with it Christianity itself. Our people, as has been openly enough declared, should be converted from the supernatural view of the world that has hitherto prevailed, to a purely natural view. No one can fail to see, and our opponents least of all, that, if this should succeed, Christianity would vanish. Let them call what they shall put in its place Christianity,— at least at first, to prevent simple souls, who are not easily freed from prejudices, from being shocked too soon,— Christianity will really no longer exist; for it is fundamentally and essentially supernatural. It is faith in an act of God, who has taken this earthly world in his grasp, and fulfilled the work of redemption. The point where the supernatural concentrates as it were, where it has its centre, is the person of Jesus Christ, the God-man. Therefore it is perfectly natural that the chief attack is directed against this point. The attack proceeds, however, according to the whole character of the present age, in historical array. The picture which the Church has hitherto made of her Head, of Christ, and has made unanimously, is represented as unhistorical. It is said to be proved, that Jesus of Nazareth did not so live and act as the Church believes. If this should be proved, it would destroy the historical foundation of Christianity; and since Christianity is not a system of doctrines, but simply faith in the redemptive act of God, that has been revealed in history, it would fall with its foundations.

Since I undertake to treat of the modern representations of the life of Jesus,—which, different as they are, have the common aim to prove the Church's representation of Christ to be unhistorical, and to set up another in its place, which is pretended to be historical,—it is necessary, for the sake of being understood, to speak still further in the way of introduction. The appearance of such works as that of Renan, and the like, naturally has a sudden effect upon any one who is not familiar with the discussions concerning the beginning of the Christian Church, which have been carried on with great warmth, but for the most part in purely scientific circles, during the last thirty or forty years. But they are not at all novel; their appearance has been long prepared for; and it is of the greatest importance in judging them to regard them in connection with their antecedents, to consider their gradual growth. In this very act there is a criticism. Every thing sudden is somewhat startling; but this effect passes away when one learns the gradual approach of the phenomenon. It gives us at the very outset a certain confidence in the Church's representation of Christ, when we look over the whole row of attempts to set it aside, and see that each new attempt begins in the same way, — to show that the preceding one is unsatisfactory. It is as if we heard at the door the feet of them who shall come in to carry out those also who lord it over the present day.

For this purpose I must lead you a generation back, to the time when the appearance of the first edition of the "Life of Jesus" by Strauss caused a commotion in our Fatherland, similar to that which the "Life of Jesus" by Renan has lately aroused in France. At that time the old rationalism had about lost its power in science. Only its last defenders occupied chairs in the university, and this was also the amount of its force in the pulpit. This old, or, as it is also called, vulgar rationalism, held to the genuineness of the Gospels (passing doubtfully over the Gospel of John, it is true), and was, on the whole, decided that they were historical. But, it said, they must be rationally interpreted. The chief rules of this rational interpretation were a many-sided accommodation on the part of the Lord, and a naturalistic explanation of the miracles. By means of these exegetical tricks, it could do away with every thing supernatural, and still get from the Gospels a perfectly natural picture of Jesus which corresponded with their rational ideas. Whatever there was in the words of the Lord that exceeded the measure of sound human reason, was explained as accommodation. It was said that in such places Jesus only accommodated himself to the ideas of his contemporaries; when, for instance, he declared himself to be the Messiah, and when he taught the doctrines of angels and devils.

Yes, all that relates to the atonement is only an accommodation to the sacrificial ideas of the Jews. The miracles are altogether natural occurrences, related in the style of Oriental fancy. If one strips off the hull of this style, and only understands how to read these Oriental stories, there remains a very simple, not at all supernatural, often indeed a very insipid, kernel within. Thus, for instance, the story of the transfiguration amounts to this. Once, while Jesus was having a consultation with two intimate, confidential friends (who, by the way, play a very large part in the rationalistic interpretations), the first rays of the rising sun shone upon him. From this the imagination of the disciples created the transfiguration, and the presence of the two intimate friends led them to imagine Moses and Elias. The turning water into wine was a wedding-joke of Jesus, who had some wine, that was kept ready, brought in at the nick of time. The shining of the heavenly hosts on the fields near Bethlehem was a phosphorescent phenomenon, if indeed it was not merely the light from a large stable-lantern, as one of the interpreters supposes. Thus the whole appearance of Jesus was thoroughly natural. He became a Jewish rabbi, the wise teacher of Nazareth, whose doctrine, if one takes a rational view of it, has always, it is true, been of great consequence; but its importance consists essentially in this, that he first taught the truths which any one can get from his own reason. It was gradually perceived, however, that all this was untenable and unsatisfactory. It could not be concealed, that the evangelists were made to say very different things from what they really said; and, though rationalism had always striven to hold fast the sinlessness of Jesus, it became clear, that the accommodation attributed to Jesus was morally equivocal, and at least a self-deception. The period of the vulgar rationalism passed by. After the first thirty years of this century, its rule was entirely overthrown. There was opposed to it, on one side, a believing theology, excited by the great experiences of the contest for freedom, and advanced by the active service of Schleiermacher; on the other side, unbelief took courses that were entirely new.

After these new roads had been pointed out for some time from different quarters, Strauss, in his "Life of Jesus," was the first to follow them out to the end. Strauss opposed both sides, both the Church doctrine and rationalism. According to his view, the Gospels contain substantially no history; neither a history of supernatural events, as the Church doctrine declares; nor a history of natural events, as rationalism declares: but merely myth, a wreath of legends which the romance of the disciples bound about the head of the Master. The prophecies of the Old Testament afforded the special occasion for this. It was supposed that these had been fulfilled in Jesus of Nazareth; and therefore tradition, with its unintentional fiction, fabricated a whole list of tales according to Old-Testament prophecies and Old-Testament models. These tales certainly have an historical appearance; but they really contain less of nothing than of history. For instance, since the legend makes Moses give water to the people, the Messiah must do more,— he gives wine. Hence the story of turning water into wine. Since Moses returns from the mountain with a shining face, the legend concerning Jesus grows to the story of the transfiguration. Thus arose all the accounts of the healing of the sick. This was expected of the Messiah; therefore it was attributed to Jesus in the legend. And since Elias had raised some one from the dead, of course the Messiah can have done no less. Take away every thing legendary, and there remains hardly any thing that is historical. The original stem, says Strauss, is so wrapped in creeping plants of legend, that it is now scarcely to be distinguished; and we really know hardly any thing more about Jesus than that he lived, taught, and finally died on the cross.

Thus the whole form of the Lord was enveloped in mythical clouds. It is no longer known who he was: this alone can be said with certainty, that he was not, as the Church believes, God become man. But Christianity, the Church, still exists: Strauss cannot deny us this. Whence has this sprung? To this question Strauss only repeats the purely negative answer,— Not from supernatural causes. Then from what natural causes? This he cannot tell; for the reiterated, monotonous derivation of the New-Testament stories from the Old-Testament models and prophecies, is far too dry to furnish the most distant idea of the actual, concrete fulness of life which then existed. By the pretended denial of the supernatural origin of Christianity, Christianity itself has become inexplicable. We are wholly in the dark; and Strauss, instead of solving a riddle for us, has given us a much harder one.

Every historical phenomenon must have a sufficient cause. To this rule, Christianity is no exception. If it is asserted that the Church is mistaken in assuming a supernatural cause, they who make this assertion cannot escape the burden of proving how Christianity sprung from merely natural causes. So long as this remains unproved, they have accomplished nothing, and can never avoid the necessity of assuming supernatural causes where natural causes are insufficient. That task is before us, to accomplish which the so-called Tübingen school worked so many years. Let us see with what result.

The late Professor Baur, of Tübingen, the chief of the Tübingen school, which also bears his name, once said, "Strauss tried to surprise the fortress, and to take it by storm; but it showed that it required a regular siege." This siege Baur undertook, with unceasing labor, with the greatest ingenuity, and with untiring endurance. The trenches were begun at a distance, to proceed gradually nearer to the heart of the fortress. The Tübingen school begins, not with the life and person of the Lord, but with the apostolic and post-apostolic times. From these times it proceeds to learn, that in the apostolic period there are traces of a twofold tendency, both among the apostles and the Church at large, — a Jewish-Christian side, and a freer Gentile-Christian side. Formerly, it was assumed that this division, broad as it was in apostolic circles, went no deeper, did not disturb the unity of the Church; that, on the contrary, the extreme Jewish-Christian party soon separated from the Church, and went into the Ebionite heresy. But the Tübingen school declares this division to have been the motive-power throughout the early times, extending far into the second century; and insists that in this contest it was that Christianity gradually freed itself from Judaism. Accordingly, the earliest history of the Church takes about the following form: The primitive Church — the original apostles, even Peter and John not excepted — was thoroughly Jewish-Christian; that is to say, the Christians were really still Jews in all their views and customs; only distinguished from the other Jews on the single point, that, while the latter still expected the Messiah, the former declared that he had already appeared in Jesus of Nazareth. In other respects, this Jewish-Christianity was based altogether upon the law and particularism: it knew as little of justification by faith, as of the spread of the kingdom of God among the Gentiles. Hence, unless another tendency had made its appearance, this Jewish Christianity would have remained a mere phenomenon within the Jewish Church. This other tendency appeared in Paul, who was the first to effect the revolution from the religion of law to the religion of freedom, from particularism to universalism. The two tendencies were directly opposed to each other, and there was no reconciliation during the apostolic period. Paul's whole life was a fight against Judaism; and, it must be added, a fight to no purpose: he was worsted by Judaism. It was in the post-apostolic period that the controversy became less intense. Each side gave up its extremes, modified itself; and, through a series of transactions, the reconciliation was conducted to perfect neutrality, to a treaty of peace, in the old Catholic Church, with the formula, — Faith and works, Peter and Paul. Most of the writings which the Church, from the standpoint of this treaty of peace, afterwards transferred back into the apostolic period, and received into the canon, are only documents of these transactions. The only writings of genuine apostolic origin are the thoroughly Jewish-Christian Revelation of John, and four Epistles of Paul (Romans, First and Second Corinthians, Galatians). All the rest are partisan writings of one or the other tendency, evidences of the conflict. *Tendency*, — that is now the magic word by which all these writings are explained. Their tendency is looked for, whether Jewish-Christian or Pauline, hostile or conciliatory, or entirely neutral; and they are ranked accordingly. The Gospels also are now no longer, as Strauss tells us, products of the unintentional fiction of legend; but plainly intentional, partisan writings of the different factions, who therein defend their views, and according to them draw the portrait of the Lord. Thus Matthew is a party-pamphlet on the Jewish-Christian side, Luke is one on the Pauline side; both, however, belonging to a certain grade of the approaching reconciliation: while Mark, the latest of the Synoptic Gospels, represents the full neutrality.

But, I hear you ask, what has all this to do with the person of Christ? Little or nothing. Schwegler, who made the first full and connected statement of the views of the Tübingen school, wrote an essay, pretending to discuss the origin of Christianity, in which he alludes to Christ, only incidentally, in a remark, saying that it is not really known who he was, and it can only be said, that he did not have a very deep influence upon his disciples. This, it is true, was afterwards modified by Baur. According to his view, Christianity did really exist in Christ: but this by no means settles the question; for then Baur discourses again about a deep gulf that lay between the life of the Lord and the apostolic period. Granted that Christianity existed in Christ, the disciples, nevertheless, were extreme Judaizers, were really still Jews and not Christians. Consequently, Christ is not the actual founder of Christianity. But who is? One thinks of Paul; but that does not suffice, for Paul also was defeated. The fact is, Christianity had no founder, and no definite beginning. It was of gradual formation: it gradually freed itself from Judaism by a series of transactions, and in this process must we seek for the true origin of Christianity, — we ourselves do not know where or how. This school, generally, does not make much account of persons and personal influence. Baur says, somewhere, " Persons are mere names, — they are merely the bearers of the ideas; and in this consists their only influence. Persons are nothing: the idea is all."

The Tübingen school has fallen to pieces, and exists no more. After the death of its master, it was outwardly broken; and since its disciples have partly strayed into extremes, and partly approached nearer to the view of the Church, it may be regarded as inwardly vanquished. The whole partisan or tendency theory — which detected everywhere about the plain and simple evangelists the most artful designs, in every line, in every omission, and in every expression — has proved to be a mere fancy; and the evangelists, whether one takes the contents of their stories to be historical or unhistorical, are admitted to have been plain, simple people, who only repeated what they found. And besides, in the present state of science, it is no longer possible to place the most of the canonical writings in so late a period as the second century. The Tübingen school, in order to gain room and time for their transactions, for the whole business of the compromise between the Judaizing and the Pauline tendencies, — which, according to them, was the process by which Christianity began, — must separate the dates of the documents of this process — the writings of the New Testament — as much as possible, and bring them down into the second century. But this has been proved to be impossible. One decade after another has been wrung from them; and, however one may stand in other respects, it can no longer be denied upon scientific grounds, that no critical arts can lead us again out of the first century. Thus has the Tübingen school been more and more hemmed in; forced back, one may say, upon the very person of Christ. It is plainly shown to be impossible to explain the origin of Christianity, without determining who Christ was; without proceeding from the proposition, that the whole movement was begun by him, and that it can only be explained by his personal life and influence.

From this review of the labors and development of the last thirty years, it may be understood why the person of Jesus appears again in the foreground; why the subject of discussion is no longer the apostolic and the post-apostolic period, but the life of Jesus. The attempt, undertaken with every scientific means, to explain Christianity in a certain sense without the person of Jesus, by a mere development of ideas, for which personality was of little importance, is to be considered thwarted. Whoever refuses to renounce that explanation is nevertheless obliged to regard the person of Jesus; he is obliged to answer the question, "What think ye of Christ? whose son is he?" He can no longer be disposed of in a single remark, as Schwegler treated him; and the gulf which Baur made between him and his apostles must be bridged over. The attack, therefore, is all the more dangerous, since it is now directed against the very heart of the Christian faith; but the change in the situation is evidence of unmistakable progress. We are at least rid of Christianity without Christ. The ground is cleared; and, though the fight is harder, the issue is fortunately nearer.

This progress is perceived at once when one goes from the older work of Strauss, and from the Tübingen school, to Renan, to the notorious work, "Vie de Jésus." The Tübingen people could not tell who was the founder of Christianity. They supposed that it really had no founder, since the person is entirely subject to the idea. But Renan makes us deal decidedly with the person of Jesus; and of nothing is Renan more sure, than that he was the founder of the new religion, — that from him it received every thing, good and bad. While Strauss left us in the dark concerning who Jesus was, since the sources seemed to him insufficient to determine that fact, Renan finds much more of history in the Gospels, — enough to describe the person of Jesus as perfectly as the person of a Cæsar or Augustus, or any other man of ancient times. His image no longer floats in mythical clouds: Renan, upon a background of landscape and history, done in a masterly way, draws it for us with sharp outlines, which at least leave nothing to be desired in clearness and decision.

I will try, in the first place, to set before you the principal features of this portrait.

Jesus was born in Nazareth, of humble parents (the account of his birth in Bethlehem and the attendant circumstances is, of course, a mere legend), and he was consequently without more education than a child of the people usually had at that time. But from the beautiful natural scenes of Galilee, which Renan so charmingly describes, and from his own heart, he forms a consciousness of God such as no one before or after him has had. Then he begins to preach in Galilee. God is our Father, and all men are brethren: this is the substance of his preaching. He prophesies a kingdom of God; but a kingdom of God which is within man, which he must create within his own heart " by the righteousness of his will and the poesy of his soul." * A pure service of God, a religion without priests and without ritual, resting wholly upon the feelings of the heart, upon imitation of God, upon the immediate communion of the consciousness with the heavenly Father, — this is the ground-plan of this kingdom of heaven. It is a perfectly new idea which thus enters the world, — the idea of a service of God based upon purity of heart and the brotherhood of man; an idea so exalted, that even now there are but few souls fit to devote themselves to it. The outlines of this idea are visible in the Sermon on the Mount, " the most beautiful code of perfect life that any moralist has traced." † The

* Vie de Jésus, p. 139 (Wilbour's Trans., p. 187).
† Vie de Jésus, p. 61 (Wilbour's Trans., p. 110).

later realistic conception of the kingdom of God is as yet totally wanting. This is a supplementary eclipse of the idea, an error, which the death of Jesus makes us forget. Nor did he at first work miracles. This was the time when the exalted idea stood forth in its purity, "some months, perhaps a year, during which God really lived upon the earth." * There were no Christians yet; but Christianity existed, and never more perfectly than at that moment. Jesus added nothing more to it: on the contrary, he only compromised the idea; " for every idea, in order to succeed, must needs make sacrifices ; none comes immaculate out of the struggle of life." † Had Jesus died then, his idea would have remained purer, and he would have been greater in the sight of God; but, unknown to men, he would have been lost in the multitude of great souls that are unknown. It is not enough to conceive a great idea: one must also make it effective. This is only possible through ways that are less pure. Certainly, if the gospel contained nothing more than several chapters of Matthew and Luke, it would be more perfect; but without miracles it would not have overcome the world.

Mark these propositions. They are the key to Renan's whole representation. The idea, which at first came forth in perfect purity, is more and more compromised,—this is essentially the whole life of Jesus. Jesus, in order to realize his idea, constantly

---

* Vie de Jésus, p. 58 (Wilbour's Trans., p. 107).
† Vie de Jésus, p. 66 (Wilbour's Trans., p. 115).

descends from the heights of the ideal, enters into real life, and finally succumbs.

The first impulse in this direction came from his meeting with John the Baptist. This personage does not appear to have had a good influence upon Jesus, who permits himself to be urged out of his own course, and follows for a time the ways of John; for he baptizes as John does,—an outer ceremony, which is not at all consistent with the pure Christianity of Renan. But the change is still deeper. From this time forward, Jesus exerts himself to realize his ideal in the world. He becomes a revolutionary character, yet one who, in the transcendental, spiritual way, desires to reform the inner world.

This brings us to the second period of his work. He now preaches the kingdom of heaven, which he himself brings. Here is a radical change of base, a revolution, which shall even include nature, and which banishes sickness and death. In the towering flight of his heroic will, he believes himself almighty, a reformer of the universe. But not through the bloody paths of political revolution shall his ideal be reached : his revolution is a moral one. There is yet no mention of the angels and the trump of the last day. The kingdom of God, realized by men among men,—this is the thought of that beautiful Galilean idyl which is played in this act of his life. Riding upon a gentle ass, by the Lake of Gennesaret, amidst the magnificent scenes of nature, surrounded by a multitude that applauds him, young fishermen his enthusiastic friends, women and children his followers, publicans and Magdalenes who found " in their conversion to the sect a ready means of reinstatement," * — thus he proceeds through the country. It is a continual holiday, an uninterrupted ecstasy ; a rural, heavenly wedding-festival.

This beautiful dream also vanishes. He is seized with the desire to go out of Galilee into Judæa, to Jerusalem, there to attack Judaism in its established fortress. There, however, he found a very different place from rustic Galilee; there he did not have fishermen and country-girls to deal with. The temple with its priests and sacrifices displeased him: he took a scourge to purify it, but he and his provincials made no impression upon the capital. Out of humor, he leaves Jerusalem. By this time he has entirely lost the Jewish faith ; his revolutionary passion burns higher and higher. The innocent aphorisms of the first period, the fine moral sermons of the second, are past. The Law must be destroyed ; he will destroy it: the Messiah has come ; he is the Messiah : the kingdom of God shall be revealed ; it is he through whom the revelation shall be made, — this is now the substance of his preaching. He knows that he shall fall a sacrifice ; but the kingdom of God is only to be gained by force. These are very different thoughts from those of the time of the Galilean idyl. The Messiah is known as the son of David: Jesus knows very well that he is not descended from

* Vie de Jésus, p. 134 (Wilbour's Trans., p. 182).

David, but he also knows that without this name he can accomplish nothing. Therefore he permits its use, — at first unwillingly; then he takes pleasure in it. Here lie the first germs of the legend, which begins to grow in his very lifetime. Miracles were regarded at that time as indispensable signs of the divine, as necessary proofs of the prophetic, calling. Jesus was confined to this alternative, — he must abandon his mission, or he must work miracles. He worked miracles, — late, to be sure, and against his will. Miracles were an obligation imposed upon him by the age in which he lived; a concession which was forced from him. Miracles were actually brought to him and put upon him. People thought that he must work miracles, and the miracles appeared. Sick persons believed that they had recovered by his touch: and he not only permitted this; he encouraged it. Very different now sounds the preaching about the kingdom of God. He now declares concerning this kingdom, that he will return upon the clouds of heaven; he talks of the day of judgment, and of the renewal of all things. From a preacher of morals, he has become an apocalyptic fanatic. His enmity towards the ruling powers grows more and more bitter; his speeches are full of a rage that has hitherto been foreign to them. His natural gentleness disappears; he becomes austere, dictatorial; he will no longer endure opposition; his words sometimes sound harsh, even *bizarre*. A crisis had come: it was time for death to loose the knot.

This occupation in Galilee lasted about eighteen months; then with the journey to Jerusalem came the final decision. His stay in Jerusalem was uncomfortable. In the discussions with the Pharisees about disputed points of the Law, Jesus did not have the superiority which on other occasions was sustained by the pure morality, that here rather placed him at a disadvantage. Jesus was no longer himself. His friends felt this; they felt it necessary that something extraordinary should occur, a great miracle, — whereupon the resurrection of Lazarus was arranged. Lazarus, pale from protracted illness, is laid in the grave, and the comedy of resurrection from the dead is played. Jesus at least knew all about it, and permitted it. He could not curb the desire of his followers for miracles. Fortunate was it that death soon restored him to the divine freedom, and delivered him from the fatal necessities of a part that could no longer be sustained.

It is unnecessary to give at length Renan's account of his death. It is sufficient to say that the resurrection is not historical. The excited Mary Magdalene believed that he had risen, and the disciples believed it with her. " Divine power of love! sacred moments, in which the passion of a hallucinated woman gives to the world a resurrected God!"* Thus Renan concludes, — a conclusion quite worthy of such a biography.

That is the life of Jesus, according to Renan. A rare picture, so strange, so different from all former

---

* Vie de Jésus, p. 308 (Wilbour's Trans., p. 357).

portraits of the Lord, that at first one stands before it in bewilderment, and must exert himself to recollect that the artist intended it to be the portrait of Jesus of Nazareth. How did Renan get the material for this strange, this perfectly new picture? Has he discovered any new authorities? No, not one. His authorities are our familiar four Gospels, to which there is only added as a fifth Gospel, as Renan expresses it, torn but still legible, the view of the locality, the view of the East, of the Holy Land, of its landscapes, of its manners and customs. He has no new authorities; but he knows how to handle the old ones, and elicit from them things which no one had ever thought of before. The truth is, that the Gospels have received from Renan an arbitrary treatment, such as no biographer ever used towards his authorities. In the first place, they are made generally uncertain. Without thorough investigation of their credibility, Renan reaches the conclusion that they contain much that is historical, but much also that is legendary. Thus he has perfect freedom in the use of them: he takes what suits him, and sets aside what does not suit his history. He recognizes, on the whole, much more history in the Gospels than Strauss and Baur. But, while he admits one story to be historical to the smallest detail, — another which stands by its side, vouched for by the same historian, is totally excluded as mere legend. Why, we ask, shall not this be true, if that is true? We seek in vain for a reply. If so much is authentic as is assumed by Renan, who is apparently struck by the liveliness and clearness of the evangelical narratives, why should not more be true? The answer to this is not always clearly expressed, but it exists essentially throughout: because nothing supernatural can be true. For this reason the Gospels are shuffled like a pack of cards; they are broken into single parts and particles, and these are put together again in a mosaic, without any regard for the chronology and the plan of the Gospels, according to an original chronology for which the authorities do not furnish the least ground. When this is not sufficient, aid is given by the imagination, which is very fertile in Renan, and supplies him with information which no authority can give.

Do you wish for examples of these performances? According to all the Gospels, Jesus meets John the Baptist before he begins his public work. Renan, on the contrary, knows of a whole period of his ministry which at that time was past. He also knows what the Lord taught and did during this period. With entire arbitrariness, this fictitious period is filled up with speeches and acts of Jesus, which are related by the evangelists as first taking place after his meeting with John the Baptist. If any thing in the life of Jesus is established, it is this, that Jesus himself instituted the Lord's Supper. If the testimony of the three evangelists is not sufficient, we have the unsuspected testimony of Paul; and it is also vouched for by the admitted, universal practice of the primitive Church. Renan, however, knows better than this. Jesus did not institute the Lord's Supper. How does Renan know this? Is it not told by the first three evangelists, whom he believes implicitly concerning other things? Renan says John does not relate it. But Renan believes John least of all: indeed, in his eyes John is the most unreliable witness; the book was not in existence until 150, and the discourses it contains are only Platonic dialogues in an entirely foreign, mythical style! And, if this view is not accepted, the silence of John nevertheless tells more in this case than the speech of the others. The treatment of the fourth Gospel is beyond measure baseless in its arbitrariness. The book is not authentic; and yet Renan uses it as a good authority whenever it suits him. To all this is added the uncontrolled, ruling, and creative imagination. It is not only said that Jesus rode on an ass through Galilee,— an incident which Renan must have got from some sixth Gospel,— but Renan also composes the whole Galilean idyl: where the wife of Pilate is minutely described for us, as she looks out of her window, and sees the charming figure of Jesus; where also brand-new speeches are put into the mouth of the Lord,— for instance, that the law is abolished, while the evangelists make him say that he has come, not to destroy, but to fulfil. That is the origin of this medley of truth and fiction, — an historical romance, a favorite kind of composition nowadays.

What is the result? Who is Jesus, according to this description? Shall I bluntly repeat it?— a fanatic, who gradually becomes an impostor, and whom death finally takes off at the earliest moment from the embarrassment of complications which he had himself prepared. Or shall I describe his progress more in detail? first, a pious, amiable fanatic, who set before himself a precious, but, alas! impracticable ideal; then a gloomier fanatic, who dreams of the trump of the judgment-day, of his second coming, of a great catastrophe and revolution of the world; then an impostor against his own will, who permits himself to be forced to one concession after another; finally, an intentional impostor. The fine words, of which Renan is so remarkable a master, are here of no avail: the things themselves speak. Decide for yourselves in this matter: if Jesus permits the name "son of David" to be given him, without contradicting it, even taking pleasure in it, although he knows that he is not descended from David, are we not already on the boundary of imposture? If, as Renan explains, he now and then used this innocent artifice,—telling his disciples about things which he had experienced in a perfectly natural way; incidents from their own lives of which he had heard, as if they had come to him by supernatural means, —what name has this artifice among honest men? He pretends to work miracles, and works none, as he well knows: what is this but imposture? And then that comedy in Bethany, in which, if he did not make the plot, he at least took part. That is really so strong a bit, that they were ashamed to dish it up for us Germans. It is wanting at least in a German edition which I have consulted.

How does Renan come to this? If I have a correct impression of his description, I believe that it is not pleasant for him to come to it: he would like to avoid it; he would like to represent the Lord as more purely moral, if he could. But, according to his presumptions, this is impossible. Others have taken the course of declaring all such things to be unhistorical: they assert that Jesus never said he should come again upon the clouds, — that this was merely a misunderstanding of the disciples; they have declared such miracles as the resurrection of Lazarus to be nothing but fiction, without even a kernel of history. This Renan cannot do; he has too much historical sense; he admits too much authentic historical tradition in the authorities to make this possible for him. But if, on the other hand, he is unable to recognize any thing supernatural in the person and the works of the Lord, there is no other course left for him than that which he has taken. If Jesus actually said that he should return upon the clouds of heaven, and this Renan does not venture to deny, what can we see in it but fanaticism if he is not the Son of God from heaven? If the Lord actually told the disciples about events in their lives which had taken place without his knowledge, and Renan must admit this on the ground of the authorities, how shall he explain it if he refuses once for all to allow a higher knowledge in Jesus, except as a little trick, an innocent deception, by which he sought to convince them? It is the same with the miracles: Renan has too much historical sense not to grant, that something must have occurred during the life of the Lord which his contemporaries at least supposed to be miracles. But, much as may be attributed to rumor and legend, it is impossible to account for all in this way. Much of it is very easily explained. The sick people believed that Jesus could heal them; and therefore they were healed, or at all events they thought they were healed. There is still a good deal left. How shall he explain that, except by the assumption of more or less intentional imposture? Take the story of the raising of Lazarus: Renan cannot explain this as nothing but rumor. Something of the kind must have occurred, which made upon the people of the time the impression of a resurrection of a dead person. What choice is there but to say either a man was actually raised from the dead, or a deception was practised? Since Renan will not say the former, he must say the latter. We may truly learn from Renan whither one is led, who, on the one hand, admits the records of the evangelists to be historical, even if it is only in their outlines, — and this must be admitted by any one who is not willing to fall into a most unscientific arbitrariness; and, on the other hand, refuses to acknowledge that Jesus is the Son of God become man. Then, it is true, one gets a mere man, but most certainly not a purely moral one, a pattern of genuine humanity; but one that is from intrinsic necessity a fanatic and an impostor.

This, then, is the author of Christianity; this the

founder of the Church! Now, I pray you, look for a moment at the facts: here is Christianity, here is the Church, here is the whole Christian life and its unfailing fruits, its blessed influences upon individuals, upon entire nations, upon all mankind. These are facts. They must have, according to reasonable thinking, a sufficient cause. Answer calmly for yourselves the question, whether this life of Jesus, as Renan tells it, is a sufficient cause; whether this Jesus of Renan can be the author of such a religion, the founder of such a Church. Is not this a supposition quite incomprehensible, quite impossible? Tell me, if you can, how it comes to pass: there lives in Palestine this Jesus, a fanatic who believes himself to be almighty, without being so; who dreams that he is the judge of the world, and is only a man; who pretends to work miracles, and works none; who at last turns impostor, and perishes, ruined by his own guilt. Twenty years after his death, the same persons who were his associates declare him to be a God, and, what is most strange, they have faith in this; then things are told of him, miracles, which never occurred. He had consented to imposture; and this is not only forgotten, but he is made the author of a religion which condemns all deception most severely: he is even made to say that lying is from the devil. There are such men as this Paul, who, whatever else may be said of him, was a sober, calm man, remarkably clear-headed, thoroughly honest; and he changes from a persecutor to his apostle. His enemies persecute him to death, accuse him before the court, make every effort in their power to destroy his followers; but there is no trace of evidence that the miracles which he told were denied by them, or that they ever attempted to prove them to be imposture, although as his contemporaries they must have had proof enough at their command. Solve for me only one of these many riddles.

Let us, however, listen to Renan himself. He perhaps has found the solution. He first complains that we always speak so rudely of lying and imposture. "It is easy for us, impotent as we are, to call this falsehood, and, proud of our timid honesty, to treat with contempt the heroes who accepted, under other conditions, the battle of life. When we shall have done with our scruples what they did with their falsehoods, we shall have the right to be severe upon them." * But, you will say, that is a justification of lying for pious purposes. Certainly it is; and it is not merely given in the heat of a moment, but just here appears Renan's whole view of life and the world. You remember the propositions which I have already quoted, that the idea cannot be realized without losing its purity. Here you have those propositions in plainer language. "Such is the feebleness of the human mind, that the best causes are ordinarily gained only for bad reasons." † "There is no great foundation which does not repose upon legend." * "All great things

---

* Vie de Jésus, p. 181 (Wilbour's Trans., pp. 227, 228).
† Vie de Jésus, p. 184 (Wilbour's Trans., p. 231).

are achieved by the people: now the people are led only by yielding to their ideas."* "He who takes humanity with its illusions, and seeks to act upon it and with it, cannot be blamed."* "The only guilt in such a case is that of humanity, which *will* be deceived."* One cannot be plainer. Here you have the proposition in its naked simplicity. The world will be deceived, therefore it is deceived; and this proposition as the foundation, as the canon and standard, of the life of Jesus! Take notice here, that these are the moral foundations of those who talk so much about morality, and plume themselves upon reducing Christianity to its simple moral principles.

There remains one more step for us to take. A man's view of the world depends upon the conception which he has of God. Let us test Renan in this deepest base. Has Renan any God left? It seems so. He certainly glorifies Jesus above all men, because he had a pure consciousness of God, such as no one before him and no one after him has ever had. Pure Christianity, according to his view, is nothing else than this preaching about God, the Father of all mankind. On the contrary, it must look suspicious when Renan explains the substance of faith as a Utopia; still more when he frequently attributes to Jesus pantheistic-colored thoughts,— when he says of him, that, according to his poetic conception, one breath of God pervades the whole universe. If we inquire, elsewhere, how Renan

* Vie de Jésus, p. 181 (Wilbour's Trans., pp. 227, 228).

expresses himself concerning this question, there can be hardly a doubt left about his real thoughts. There is an article in the "Revue des Deux Mondes"* for 1863, a letter from Renan to Berthelot, the chemist, which in its expressions concerning the essence of God is in many respects obscure and indistinct: but this much is clear, that Renan's God is not the free personal God of the Scriptures; not the Creator of the world, the Father of our Lord Jesus Christ. It is evident that his views are strongly tinged with pantheism. The consciousness of God, therefore, which Jesus had was nothing: Renan has another. There is no such heavenly Father as Jesus declares,—at least Renan does not believe in him; and, although he occasionally acts as if he believed in this heavenly Father, it is fair enough to suppose, that, according to his previously developed propositions, this is only an accommodation to the notions of the people whom he desires to influence. The guilt of such an accommodation falls, of course, not upon him, but upon the people who still hold fast the old ideas. The time will come, perhaps, when this veil also may be dropped, and, instead of the Father of our Lord Jesus Christ, one can openly preach the Pan-God to the people.

Renan in one place describes in vivid colors the heights of Nazareth, and the view one has from there of the beautiful outlines of Carmel falling precipitously to the sea, of the mountains of Gilboa, the gracefully rounded Tabor, and, far beyond, the

* Tome 47, Livraison 15. Octobre, 1863.

valley of the Jordan. Then he breaks forth with these spirited words: "If ever the world, still Christian, but having obtained a better idea of what constitutes respect for origins, shall desire to substitute authentic holy places for the mean and apocryphal sanctuaries which were seized upon by the piety of the barbarous ages, it is upon this height of Nazareth that it will build its temple." * That will probably be the temple where Sakya-Muni, Mohammed and Jesus, whom Renan is so fond of classing together, shall peacefully receive a common veneration, and mankind, free at last, shall worship the God of Renan.

Is it an accident that Renan places this temple just at Nazareth? Then it is certainly a remarkable accident. For you remember the reception Jesus met with in this same Nazareth, and what we find written of Nazareth: "They were offended at him," and "He marvelled because of their unbelief."

* Vie de Jésus, p. 21 (Wilbour's Trans., p. 71).

SECOND DISCOURSE.

"THE CHARACTER OF JESUS PORTRAYED,"[*]
BY SCHENKEL.

"A NEW LIFE OF JESUS,"[†] BY STRAUSS.

THE "Life of Jesus" by Renan, which was discussed at our last meeting, has had a wide influence. Translated into almost every language of civilized Europe, it has been spread in many thousands of copies; mostly, however, among the nations speaking the Romanic languages, and within the domain of the Romish Church, to which Renan originally belonged. It might easily be shown, that the whole character of the book exactly corresponds to this sphere. It may be remarked, by the way, that the wide circulation of the book in Roman-Catholic countries, the eagerness with which it has there been, as it were, devoured, is also a proof that the popular faith within the Romish church is not in so good a state as is often declared; that the unchristianizing of the masses, especially of the educated classes, is going on there, too, to a greater degree

[*] Title of Furness's Translation.
[†] Title of Authorized Translation.

perhaps than with us, although it is not so conspicuous by the side of the apparently greater power of the Church. The book has been generally offered to our German people in editions which omit, not only what there is of rather learned matter in the original, but also the many too absurdly frivolous assertions, a sample of which I cited in my last discourse. It was clearly seen, however, that a different kind of viand was required for us Germans; and in consequence of the excitement caused by Renan, and by the great effect of his book, attempts were made to supply our wants. Strauss, it is true, had already decided to prepare a new edition of his "Life of Jesus" for the German people, and had prepared part of it before the work of Renan appeared, — another sign of how much of this thing lay in the air; but Schenkel was first incited by the appearance of Renan's work to write his "Character of Jesus Portrayed."

He directly says, in the Preface of his book, that the sensation caused by Renan's "Life of Jesus" forcibly reminded him "of the necessity of meeting the deep want of our time, which demands a genuinely human, truly historical representation of Jesus."* For this purpose Schenkel proposes not to write precisely a Life of Jesus, but only to portray the "Character of Jesus." But the book which bears this title is really a Life of Jesus. Schenkel tells us the whole life of the Lord, from his birth to his death; he gives, on the whole,

* Schenkel's Characterbild, S. iv. (Furness's Trans., vol. i. p. xxiv.)

what one expects from a Life of Jesus. But he gained this advantage through the title, — he was not bound to deal impartially with every detail; an advantage which he has known how to use in the controversies that have arisen over his book.

If I must begin again by giving you a brief summary of the contents of this book, by trying to copy the chief features of the picture which Schenkel has sketched, I must also begin with a complaint. Coming from Renan to Schenkel, one misses at once the clear and decided lines with which Renan draws the portrait of Jesus. With Schenkel, every thing is fleeting and misty. With Renan you always know your bearings, but with Schenkel it is often impossible to tell where you are; and, when you have taken great pains to extract from the plentiful words his real opinion, you must afterwards observe with astonishment that you have entirely misunderstood him. Take a single instance of this. Friend and enemy had understood from his book, that Schenkel denied the actual resurrection of Jesus, — his friends with gratification, for they inferred from this that he had now broken entirely with the faith of the Church; his opponents with indignation, for they made this very denial of the resurrection the chief reproach against him. All at once Schenkel comes out, and complains that he has been entirely misunderstood: he by no means denied the resurrection; he did not make it, as his opponents asserted (not only his opponents, his friends likewise), a mere spiritual occurrence in the souls of the disciples; but he plainly recognized the reality of the appearance of the risen Jesus as the actual manifestation of his surviving personality in its transformed and glorified state. It is certainly unfortunate when any one expresses himself so indistinctly concerning such an important matter, that his readers entirely misunderstand him.

He is therefore in an awkward situation who has to copy the picture which Schenkel has drawn. It is hard to understand it correctly, and it is still harder to describe it to another. He has to represent this indistinctness, this variableness, and yet say what Schenkel really means. The attempt must be made; but I beg you not to blame me if the picture proves to be rather poor. The cloud of words with which Schenkel envelops the particular features, I certainly cannot furnish.

Jesus, the son of Joseph the carpenter, of Nazareth (Schenkel also sets aside the supernatural birth as a legend), was a child of the people, and grew up in narrow circumstances. This was just the right preparation for him, the future man of the people. The strength of his religious feelings showed itself very early; especially when, a boy twelve years old, he attended for the first time the feast at Jerusalem. His relation to John the Baptist is to be conceived as totally different from the representation of it given by the evangelists. John's attempt to cause a moral revival of his people was wholly a mistake. John is the man who puts new cloth on an old garment. Therefore the ways of Jesus soon separate from those of John. It is true that his Messianic calling was not yet clear to Jesus; but this was clear, that the theocracy possessed no power for reviving the people; that an act of God was necessary to do it: and he foreboded at least that this divine act should proceed from himself.

He consequently comes forth as a teacher, with the sermon, "'The time is fulfilled;' i.e., the old time of the theocracy, of ceremonial tutelage, and of the religion of forms and formulas," * — this old time is past, the kingdom of God is at hand. Repentance is the condition of admission into it. Jesus comes forth, not as the Messiah, but as the founder of a new communion of true Israelites, independent of the old theocratic conditions. He collects the first disciples as a nucleus of this, and tries to exert an influence, especially among the middle classes of the people, in the places about the Lake of Gennesaret. In Capernaum, he performs the first act which appears to the people to be a miracle. He heals one who is possessed, — possessed with a devil. According to Schenkel's view, this person was not possessed: that was merely imagined by the superstition of the age, concerning which it was not the mission of Jesus to enlighten the people. It is also not certain that the man was healed for ever; but Jesus quieted his convulsions by taking hold of him kindly, and speaking to him in a comforting way. He was now regarded by the people

---

* Schenkel's Char., S. 41 (Furness's Trans., vol. i. p. 92).

as a worker of miracles. He had this reputation without being one. Schenkel admits, that Jesus, though it was a disagreeable and unwilling task, healed sick persons by his comforting words and kind touch; but his power can be psychologically explained, not as a miracle, but as a natural gift. Real miracles, rays of his divine nature, Schenkel decidedly denies. What was supposed to be miracle, all happened within the limits of nature. In this way, a whole list of miracles are naturally explained. What cannot be explained in this way, even by Schenkel, is supposed to be either wholly or partially legend, based upon some natural event which afterwards received legendary embellishment, and became a miracle. For instance, the miracle at the wedding in Cana. Here it is only historical that Jesus went to the wedding, and thought it not unbecoming to attend to getting the wine that was wanted. In after times, however, it was thought that this was unbecoming, and the history was twisted into a legend, that Jesus procured the wine by a miracle of almighty power.

Thus passes the first period of the work of Jesus. The opposition of the hierarchical party drives him farther. The orthodox, scholastic theologians, the party of the high-churchmen,—thus Schenkel gladly designates the Scribes and Pharisees,—are offended because he breaks the Sabbath. Thereupon he proclaims freedom of worship, and appears as the representative of true human worth and eternal human rights. This completed, inwardly, the breach with the high-churchmen. In controversy with them, there had dawned upon Jesus " the conviction that the eternal Truth, which is from our Father in heaven, and which is the central life of things, had embodied itself anew in him directly and originally; whilst all the learning of the schools, and all priestly mediation and ceremonial observances, were but as a gold-fringed covering, hiding from sight all that is imperishable in the divine, all that is real in humanity." — " Ignorant obedience, or willing love, in the domain of religion and morality, — this was now the question." *

Jesus did not even yet presume to be the Messiah, but the deliverer, the liberator, of his people. The opposition to him gradually cleared his views, and he took an important step in the direction of establishing a new Israelitish religious communion (it was nothing more as yet), by selecting the twelve, and sending them forth. Therein lay a germ, that was to grow much greater. The establishment of the true Israel, this was the next object of Jesus' work. But a kingdom of the Spirit, of truth, of righteousness, of love, that has its place within men, is bound by no external statutes; is not dependent upon traditions and ceremonies, upon forms and formulas, — such a kingdom belongs to no single nation, but to mankind itself. Consequently, Jesus looked towards the Gentile world. He visited the region about Tyre and Sidon, and went to Cæsarea Philippi. This was not precisely a missionary journey: its

---

* Schenkel's Char. S. 66 (Furness's Trans., vol. i. pp. 146, 147).

object was rather to test the susceptibility of the Gentile world.

Upon his return, he utters the decisive word: he declares himself to be the Messiah. This must have been hard for him to do, for he knew that the task of the Messiah in the Old Testament was very different from his own; namely, to exalt the priestly rule of Israel to the dominion of the world, the Old-Testament theocracy to the religion of the world, while he wished to found a spiritual kingdom. He also knew that he could not fulfil the Messianic expectations of the people. Nevertheless he declared himself to be the Messiah. He was obliged to do this; for it was the only way to accomplish his purpose with a large part of the people. He was, consequently, obliged to consent to the application of Old-Testament Messianic ideas to his person, and at the same time to try to clear them of the impure elements attached to them, in order thus to fulfil them in their true sense. The fulfilment of the old covenant in his person was, it is true, the non-fulfilment of all the theocratic expectations. A suffering Messiah was, to the Jews, a contradiction; and yet it was necessary that he should become a suffering Messiah. Only in suffering could his destiny be fulfilled; suffering was to become the true sanction of his redeeming mission.

The departure to Jerusalem begins the last period in the life of the Lord,— the school of sorrow, the completion of his work. The entry into Jerusalem brings on the actual decision. By this he put arms into his enemies' hands. He came out openly as Messiah, not merely by entering the city in this character, but by the more conspicuous Messianic act of purifying the temple, by which he wished to show that this house of stone was devoted to destruction; that the destruction of the theocratic dominion and the external temple-service was already an actual fact. He wished to prove thereby his right to set up, in place of this temple of stone, which was desecrated by its own keepers, the new, great, spiritual temple of the nations. He thereupon proclaimed himself as the Messiah of a spiritual kingdom of God. His enemies were now able to prosecute him. Jesus knew that he had transgressed the letter of the antiquated law. Treachery then delivered him into the hands of his enemies. His death became the source of blessing and honor. The merciful love, the representative of which he died, arraigned the heartless law whose letter had put him to death. This law now came upon the bench of the accused, and with it the whole theocratic institution. The hierarchy was now judged, her law condemned; her formalism had become an abomination through the cross, which had been lifted up as the symbol of innocence, purity, truth, justice, love, and freedom. Thus is his death the expiation for the sins of the world. This it was, because through its blessed results the operation of the law was abolished; because through it there came to mankind the knowledge that God does not apply to sin the standard of the dead letter of prescription. The dead Christ is also the eternally living: he lives in his people. The living Christ is the Spirit of the Church. He lives in all those in whom his word has become spirit and life.

Schenkel claims that this representation of his gives a truly historical and genuinely human portrait of Jesus. The claim is the more significant, since the Church, according to Schenkel's view, has never had such a portrait of Jesus. Never, I say; for even the oldest representations of the life of Jesus, our Gospels, are neither truly historical nor genuinely human: even in them the miraculous legend has the preponderance. The Jewish-Christian party fought valiantly against the deification of Jesus, but in vain. They were unable to prevent the formation of the dogma of the God-man with his two natures, — one divine and one human. Such a twofold being is wholly unhistorical; and from this standpoint a genuinely human portrait of Jesus cannot be obtained. The reformers took this catholic dogma without testing it. They did not dare (from fear of the results, Schenkel thinks) to subject it to a searching revision, — in Schenkel's eyes a grievous mistake, which has grievously revenged itself. Rationalism first attempted to understand the person of Jesus as human; but the rationalistic portrait of Christ is unsatisfactory: it leaves the feelings cold, the imagination empty, the disposition indifferent. We cannot believe in this rationalistic Christ. Schleiermacher went a step farther: he drew such a portrait of Christ as he needed for his own religious wants. But his Christ had a great defect: he is no Christ for the people; not the Christ " as he went about and taught and labored among the people, and as, for the people, he suffered and died."* The want remains unsatisfied. The Church exists more than eighteen hundred years; sees in this Christ her Head, her Lord, her source of life; her religious services, her doctrine, her whole life, are concerned with this Christ: but, strange to say, she has not had a truly historical, genuinely human portrait of her Lord until to-day. Schenkel has tried to satisfy this great want. Verily, if he had succeeded, we should have to date a new era in the history of the Church from the day on which his " Character of Jesus " made its appearance; and Schenkel would have rendered the Church a greater service than Luther, or any of the other great men whom she venerates as her human teachers. Let us not be prevented by the greatness of the claims he advances from calmly examining them. Schenkel, it is true, offers his " Character of Jesus " only as an attempt, however surely convinced he may be that it is a successful attempt.

One word before we begin. There is a difficulty in expressing one's self exactly about Schenkel. The position he has taken towards the questions of the day, and the part he has played in the ecclesiastical controversies of late years, are apt to make judgment upon his book seem clouded by partisan-

---

* Schenkel's Char., S. 8 (Furness's Trans., vol. i. p. 14).

ship. I wish, therefore, to expressly state, that we now have to deal, not with Schenkel the Church politician, but with Schenkel the historian. The question before us, which we wish to consider with perfect impartiality, is this: whether his "Character of Jesus" is truly historical.

This requires, in the first place, that the picture be taken from the authorities. Truly historical treatment of the authorities is the first claim which we have the right to make upon an historical representation. Schenkel especially prefers the Gospel of Mark. This, he thinks, gives the record that was nearest to the scene of the Saviour's life. Mark composed it from Peter's oral discourses between 45 and 58, only about twenty years after the Lord's death, and in the very lifetime of Peter. If it is admitted that these records were made with great accuracy from Peter's discourses, as Schenkel expressly acknowledges, then we have in the second Gospel an authority as good as could be desired. Schenkel, to be sure, supposes that we do not possess the second Gospel as it came from the hand of the author: the original Mark has been revised, but this revision has not altered its essential contents. Schenkel lays Mark at the foundation: his "Character of Jesus" is intended to be a representation of the life of Jesus, based upon the second Gospel. Is he right in this? Is the view just presented concerning Mark and its relation to the other Gospels correct? I am the less inclined to dispute about it with Schenkel, since the substance of this view was not invented by him, but is borrowed from his colleague, Holtzmann. Grant it all for a moment; then certainly Schenkel's representation must agree substantially with that of Mark; his portrait of Christ, with the portrait which Mark gives. Is this the fact? You will at once reply, No: the Christ of Mark is wholly different from that of Schenkel. Take a single point, the miracles, — what a difference! Schenkel asserts that in Mark the miraculous part is less prominent than in the other Gospels, and this he adds to the arguments for its greater age. But this is simply not true. Read Matthew, and then read Mark: you will find no difference in this respect. In one, as in the other, the whole work of the Lord is pervaded by miracles, the whole coloring of the picture is supernatural. How does Schenkel reconcile his position with these facts?

Schenkel replies that the occurrence of miracles may be explained by a twofold reason. In the first place, Mark freely worked over the discourses of Peter, and wrote his Gospel under the influence of the oral tradition, and the need of miracles felt by the apostolic Church; and Peter himself may have represented, according to Old-Testament models, many an evangelical incident in a miraculous light. In the next place, the reviser of the original Gospel of Mark inserted here and there among the earlier accounts the later conceptions, although the special cases where this was done cannot now be precisely ascertained. You observe, in the first place, that Schenkel, after announcing only two reasons, really gives three; for, besides the part of Mark himself and of his reviser, a share of the guilt is imputed, by the way, in a parenthesis, to Peter. Who of the three is the chief offender? This Schenkel declines to ascertain. He contents himself with having thrown suspicion upon these three men, by the general assertion, that they introduced the legend of miracles into the record. I fear, however, that we shall be neither willing nor able to content ourselves with this general aspersion.

If the subject of dispute were nothing more than that here and there a slight miraculous touch had been added, now and then a story had been embellished with miracles, or had been put in a miraculous light, the matter might drop. But this is not the case: the question concerns a number of the greatest miracles, which Schenkel (here he is helped by the fact that he writes only a Character, not a Life, of Jesus) passes over in partial silence. There is the miracle of the loaves and fishes, the stilling of the tempest, the raising of Jairus's daughter from the dead. The whole record is saturated with miracles; the person of Jesus is placed wholly in a miraculous light; which of the three has done this? Schenkel speaks of Peter only incidentally: he does not count him with the others. He is really not to be thought of; the miraculous tales could not come from him. Take a few examples: The Lord provided food for the people in the wilderness, Schenkel says, in an entirely natural way: did Peter, then, tell the story as if Jesus had increased the bread miraculously? The Lord, on a certain occasion, showed himself more courageous than old sailors (another similar interpretation of Schenkel's): did Peter, then, make out of this the story of the stilling of the tempest? In the house of Jairus, no one was raised from the dead: did Peter, then, tell that story? This is impossible. We must release Peter: he cannot be the guilty one. Nor is there any better reason for accusing the reviser. If he were responsible for all that is miraculous, which according to Schenkel is legend, he would not only have altered essentially the original Mark: he would have created an entirely new picture of Christ. But that is not the opinion of Schenkel, or of his pioneer, Holtzmann: it would be an utterly untenable theory. Schenkel does not regard the reviser as the really guilty one. He only inserted here and there the later conceptions. No one therefore remains, but Mark himself. This surely contradicts what Schenkel has previously told us, — that Mark took down the discourses of Peter with great accuracy. We would nevertheless consent to the contradiction, if we only gained our object. But, instead of this, we find a new riddle. Mark takes notes of Peter's discourses, and makes out of them something wholly different, wholly new; gives to the natural events reported by Peter a miraculous character, creates an entirely new picture of Christ! Is that conceivable? What kind of a man must Mark have been to do it?

And, besides, this does not happen long years afterward: it takes place immediately afterward, in the very lifetime of Peter. What must Peter have said, if he ever saw or heard of this book? He had related, that the Lord fed the people in a natural way; and out of this his interpreter makes the miracle of the loaves and fishes. He had related, that the Lord showed himself courageous during a storm at sea; and here he reads that the Lord stilled the tempest. He never told about raising any one from the dead; and yet here is the story in this book, composed of his discourses. Indeed, this is more than strange: it is inconceivable. There is no escape from the difficulty. Schenkel has made a general statement of reasons for us, to show how the miraculous legends came into the record; but his explanation answers only so long as we are content with indistinctness. When we try to take fast hold of any single point, we grasp at nothing. As long as Schenkel is unable to explain definitely how such very unhistorical things have come into this excellent historical authority, so long must we dispute his right to use it as he does, — now to accept its contents as historical, now to reject them as unhistorical. That is uncritical ambiguity. He is obliged either to accept the miracles which he doubts, or to reject as unreliable an authority which relates such unhistorical things in an inexplicable way.

The matter looks still worse when we examine it in detail. Schenkel, with a readiness which calls to mind the most flourishing times of the old rationalism, can explain many of the miraculous stories as perfectly natural. For instance, it is recorded that the Lord healed a leper. Schenkel knows that in this case comforting words and a kind touch are not sufficient. They have never yet cured a bad disease of the skin. He supposes that the sick man was already essentially cured when Jesus said to him, "Be thou clean." Here we see the regular rationalistic trick of explaining, or rather of inlaying, for the evangelist says nothing of the sort: it is Schenkel alone who inserts this, without considering what an equivocal part Jesus is made to play in healing over again, or in pretending to heal, a person who had been already cured of his sickness.

This convenient trick, however, is not sufficient to account for all the miracles. There still remain records of miracles which cannot be disposed of in this way. Schenkel, accordingly, undertakes a division. He strips off all that is miraculous as a later addition, and leaves, as a truly historical kernel, an entirely natural event. In order not to use new instances constantly, I will again take as an example the miracle of the loaves and fishes. Schenkel sets aside the story, that Jesus miraculously fed thousands of people with a few loaves; but he holds, as truly historical, that Jesus once fed the people in the desert. This was done by no miracle, but by carefully arranging that the disciples should procure food. When the food was brought, Jesus distributed it among the people, after making a prayer of thanksgiving. From the impression left by this event, in connection with the Lord's teaching concerning the spiritual food, which he himself compared with the manna that sustained the people in the wilderness, the exaggerating, miracle-seeking legend constructed the story of a miraculous provision of bodily food. Then it is historical: it really happened, that Jesus fed the people in the wilderness, since, after a prayer of thanksgiving, he had food dispensed to them by his disciples. But how does Schenkel know this? From Mark, will be the reply. Yes; but Mark says, clearly and distinctly, that the feeding was miraculous. If Schenkel believes one part of this story, why does he not believe the other? If Mark is such an untrustworthy witness, that he relates a miracle when none has occurred, I cannot understand how Schenkel can treat him as such a trustworthy witness as to accept, upon his testimony, all the rest of the story, to the very details of the prayer of thanksgiving and the dispensing of the food by the disciples. I am aware that an historian can doubt particulars and secondary things in what is told by his authority, and still hold the substance to be well founded; but here the matter stands just the other way. By discarding the miracle of the story, Schenkel discards the substance of it,—the chief point, the very thing for the sake of which it was told. Can you suppose that Peter and the other apostles told their congregations such natural tales, as that the Lord once distributed bread in the wilderness, that he once showed himself courageous on the sea, etc.? Is it not the miracles for whose sake the stories are always told? It is an extremely hazardous proceeding to reject the real point of a story as unhistorical, and to hold fast subordinate points. The chief matter drags with it the by-matters irrecoverably into destruction.

But, says Schenkel, improbable as it is that the history is true as it stands, it is equally improbable that all of it has been invented. To this I reply, in the first place, Why not? When the chief thing, the miracle, has once been invented, or has originated in a change from a spiritual to a sensuous idea, why cannot the details be also invented? Is the fabricating legend so unproductive? Where does legend exhibit any thing so bare and cold and colorless? Does it not always tell its tales with life-like distinctness, and with details full of color? In the next place, I reply: We can just as fairly reverse the matter, and say of the miracle what Schenkel says of his alleged natural kernel, — that cannot have been invented. Who will then decide what can or cannot have been invented? Schenkel says of one thing, others say of another thing,— That cannot have been invented. These are merely subjective opinions, nothing more. Schenkel once said against Strauss, "If so much is historical as he admits, then still more must be historical." Precisely the same objection can be made to Schenkel; or we can reverse it, and say, as Strauss says, If so much is unhistorical as Schenkel admits, then still more must be unhistorical. It is ambiguity in criticism to stop short where Schenkel does. It is mere arbitrariness, not scientific criticism, to say, So far I believe Mark; so far I do not believe him. He must either, with Strauss, reject the whole as unhistorical; or, with the Church, accept the whole as historical.

The same arbitrariness is repeated in his treatment of the other Gospels. Thus, to take an instance from Luke, Schenkel explains the whole story of the infancy as fiction; but he retains the story about Jesus, when a boy of twelve in the temple, as having really happened. For both stories we have the same authority. What right, then, has Schenkel to reject one story and to retain the other? It will be said, The one, the story of the infancy, is full of miracles; the other, the story of the visit of Jesus, when a boy of twelve, to the temple, is thoroughly natural. I will not speak of the fact, that Schenkel is first obliged to extract the miracle from the second story by the arts of natural explanation: I will grant that at once. But I ask, Is it criticism to reject the first story, and to accept the second upon such ground? Is it not dogmatic presumption? According to Schenkel's dogmatic presumption, there can be no miracle, consequently the birth of Jesus cannot have taken place as Luke relates it, therefore the story is not authentic. On the other hand, what is related of Jesus, when a boy of twelve, can have happened; therefore it is authentic. Here we see the treatment of the authorities, as it lies at the foundation of Schenkel's representation. What agrees with his dogmatic presumptions; what fits into the image of Christ that he has made for himself; what, in his opinion, cannot have been invented; what, in his view, bears the stamp of authenticity,—that is historical: all else is not.

This proceeding reaches its climax in the treatment of the fourth Gospel. According to Schenkel, this cannot have been written by John. It contradicts the other Gospels in many places; it contains many historical and geographical errors, and therefore cannot have been written by an inhabitant of Palestine. The discourses of Jesus contained in it are profound, but obscure and enigmatical, not popular: the historical Jesus cannot have discoursed as the fourth Gospel represents. The fourth Gospel, from beginning to end, abandons the ground of history, and places itself upon a speculative standpoint. The history, regarded from this standpoint, has experienced all kinds of transformations, which have not been able to escape the acuteness of Schenkel. Thus the fourth Gospel says, The mother of Jesus stood under the cross, and from the cross the Lord spoke to her the familiar words. Schenkel, on the contrary, asserts, The mother could not endure the sight of her crucified son; and that story arose (was invented accordingly) from the desire to have, in the mother's constancy at the cross, an expiation for her former indifference to the gospel. And since the evangelist, in the story about the first miracle at the wedding in Cana, had recorded a harsh word spoken by Jesus to his mother, he would gladly end his life with a word of kindness. On the other hand, the words by which the Lord commends his spirit into the Father's hands, are omitted by the author of the fourth Gospel, because they do not agree with his idea of Jesus. If Jesus, according to the introduction of the Gospel, is the Word become flesh, of equal birth with God, he cannot thus commend his spirit into the hands of the Father.

We should suppose that such a transformation of the history, made from a speculative standpoint in the second century (110-120, Schenkel thinks), could not serve as an authority, and that Schenkel would have to leave the fourth Gospel out of sight in portraying his character. Far from it: on the contrary, without the fourth Gospel, the portrait of the Lord would lack "the unfathomable depth, the inaccessible height."* Jesus was not in reality, but in truth, such as the fourth Gospel describes him. Although it was not written by John, there lie at the foundation of the fourth Gospel accounts which come from John; and these Schenkel, of course, is able to find out, in spite of the transformation which this history has experienced from a speculative standpoint. As you please, therefore, it is both genuine and not genuine, Johannine and not Johannine, true and not true. Schenkel gains thereby the ability to use it as he pleases, to take what fits into his image of Christ, and to leave out what does not fit.

* Schenkel's Char., S. 25 (Furness's Trans., vol. i. p. 46).

Look at a few examples of this kind. The conversation of Jesus with the Samaritan woman certainly cannot have taken place as John relates it. Time and place are wrongly given; it describes Jesus as omniscient when he was not; it alludes to the relations of the Jews to the Samaritans, in such a way as to betray in the author an ignorance of their actual relations, inconceivable in a born Jew; the words of Jesus concerning the worship of God represent him in a wholly incorrect position towards the Old-Testament law. In spite of all this, we soon hear, to our great amazement, that in its main substance the story is not invented, but bears the seal of trustworthiness. The riddle is easily solved. That "loftiest plea for toleration," * which is found in this conversation, the "largeness of heart," † in the declaration of the character of the true worship of God, — could not be left out of Schenkel's portrait of Christ. Here therefore, in the midst of all that is unhistorical, is found a bit of history. In his enthusiasm over this largeness of heart, Schenkel forgets, that, a hundred and odd pages before, he adduced this same saying concerning the worship of God as a proof that the fourth Gospel puts Jesus in a position towards the law which differs entirely from the representation of the other three Gospels, and is therefore false. The same course is pursued towards the record of the washing of the disciples'

---

* Schenkel's Char., S. 125 (Furness's Trans., vol. ii. pp. 82, 83).

† "Grossartigen Weitherzigkeit." Schenkel's Char., S. 125 (Furness's Trans., vol. ii. p. 83).

feet. We learn that the fourth Gospel has arranged the events of the last evening from a speculative point of view. On that evening certainly, the washing of the disciples' feet cannot have taken place. Then perhaps the author invented it from his speculative point of view? Not at all: the washing of the disciples' feet serves so excellently to humble all priestly pride, it is such an indispensable feature in Schenkel's portrait, that here again, in spite of every thing, truly historical recollection must be recognized. The same treatment of the authorities prevails throughout. What suits Schenkel's portrait is genuine; what does not suit it is not genuine.

We are then led to the unexpected result, that, in several instances where the first three Gospels are in error, the correct account is found in the fourth Gospel; that even Mark, at other times so much preferred, must consent to be corrected by this Gospel treatise of the second century. The discourse in the sixth chapter of John furnishes us with an historical sign, that the miracle of the loaves and fishes, as related in the first three Gospels, did not take place. Comparing the Lord's discourses, as given by the first three evangelists, concerning the last things, with the final discourses of Jesus in the thirteenth and fourteenth chapters of John's Gospel, Schenkel gives John the preference. He, and not the other evangelists, has repeated the true substance of the Lord's discourses concerning the last things. All this in spite of the fact, that Jesus, according to Schenkel, cannot have made such long speeches during the last evening; in spite of the fact, that these discourses serve at other times as proof that this Gospel is not genuine. His decision in these instances also rests upon merely subjective ground. Schenkel needs the discourse in the sixth chapter of John, about the bread of heaven, to explain the rise of the legend of the loaves and fishes; and he does not like the realism of the Lord's discourses about the last things in the first evangelists, so well as the supposed spiritualistic idea of John.

This may suffice. And I may add, as the result of our examination, that Schenkel's treatment of the authorities is thoroughly uncritical and unhistorical, full of ambiguity, conformed to dogmatic presumptions and subjective arbitrariness. What would be said if any one were to treat in this way the authorities for the history of Luther or of Frederic II.?

If we now pass on to consider what it is that Schenkel gets in this way, it is clear that the gist of his whole representation is the development of the Messianic consciousness of Jesus. Jesus was not conscious of being the Messiah at his first appearance, but came gradually to this consciousness under the opposition of the high-church party. According to the Gospels, to be sure, this is not true. Schenkel must reject direct testimony upon this point, — even that of his highly respected Mark, according to which Jesus came forth fully conscious of being the Messiah. Let us overlook this, however, and ask whether this representation is possibly historical. Not as Messiah did Jesus appear, but as deliverer, as saviour of his people, as founder of a new religious communion; or he foreboded at least that the revival of the nation's life should proceed from him. But according to the prophets, according to the hopes then living in the Jewish people, the Messiah should be all these things. Could Jesus think that he was called to revive his people; could he believe himself to be the saviour, the deliverer of the people, the founder of a new religious communion,—without at once recognizing himself as the Messiah? This seems utterly impossible. Schenkel himself could not avoid this difficulty. He thinks, however, that he can solve it by representing the Messianic hope, not merely as it then lived in the people, but also as it was originally in the prophecies of the Old Testament; as one which aimed only at external dominion, at the spread of the theocracy over the whole earth. For this reason, he thinks, Jesus could not believe himself to be the Messiah; he was obliged rather to oppose most decidedly these Messianic hopes. Let it be granted for a moment,—what I do not otherwise admit,— that these hopes were solely national and theocratic: this did not prevent Jesus afterwards, in Schenkel's opinion, from declaring himself to be the Messiah; why then should it have prevented him in the beginning? He could have applied the pure meaning of these promises to himself at first, as well as at last, when Schenkel provides for it. And even if it is admitted that he could not have done it, because of reasons that are not made clear to us, no one can deny that Jesus had to accommodate himself to these hopes; and at the beginning too, unless we assume that he came forth without knowing what he wanted. That was unavoidable. If he could not have believed himself to be the Messiah, he would necessarily have been sure that he was not the Messiah; and we should thus reach the conclusion, which even Schenkel would like to evade, — namely, that Jesus confessed at first that he was not the Messiah, but was afterwards forced to the directly opposite confession. This is perplexing; but it is not so perplexing as the description of the way in which opposition to the hierarchy, and to the nature of the law, gradually led the Lord to a clear consciousness of his call to be the Messiah. Since Jesus, at the time of his baptism, was convinced " that the theocracy was no longer equal to the work of regenerating the Israelitish people;"* since, in the solitude of the wilderness, he could think of no way " but to break entirely with the theocracy; to arm himself for a life-and-death struggle," † — we should suppose that all was decided; and we are at a loss when it is afterwards asserted, as if for the first time, that "the rupture was unavoidable." ‡ If Jesus, at the commencement of his work, abandoned all respect for the theocracy, and permitted the dis-

---

* Schenkel's Char., S. 35 (Furness's Trans., vol. i. p. 74).
† Schenkel's Char., S. 40 (Furness's Trans., vol. i. p. 90).
‡ Schenkel's Char., S. 62 (Furness's Trans., vol. i. p. 140).

ciples intentionally to break the Sabbath, Schenkel is right in saying " the opposing forces on both sides had reached their acme ;" * but it is hard to find out where a further development was to come from. If Jesus, in the initiatory discourse in the Sermon on the Mount, had " solemnly withdrawn himself from all living connection with the Jewish hierarchy and theology," † what is meant by saying that afterwards, for the first time, " he changed to an attitude of open and vehement attack ?" ‡ I am still less able to understand how all this can have served to clear his Messianic consciousness.

In one word, the whole development is mere show. There is no real development there. This will be still more evident if we compare Schenkel with Renan. In Renan we have a real development at the cost of introducing the factor of sin into the life of Jesus. Jesus sins, and is ruined. Schenkel shrinks from saying this. His Jesus must not sin, must not incur guilt; but he is nevertheless supposed to have developed just as other great men have done. This is a mere show of development. It must not be overlooked, that the comparison in one respect results in Schenkel's favor. It must be acknowledged, — and I wish distinctly to declare it, — that in him there is none of Renan's frivolity. He is evidently concerned to represent Jesus as morally pure, — yes, as sinless. But it is equally clear that

---

* Schenkel's Char., S. 65 (Furness's Trans., vol. i. p. 145).
† Schenkel's Char., S. 74 (Furness's Trans., vol. i. p. 164).
‡ Schenkel's Char., S. 179 (Furness's Trans., vol. ii. p. 195).

he does not succeed in this. He feels that, in an entirely sinless Jesus, the kind of development which he wishes to represent is impossible : therefore he discourses about great inner struggles and storms, which Jesus is supposed to have experienced, about great temptations which he had to overcome. He thus puts the sinlessness in doubt; for where inner storms and temptations are, there is sin. This also is mere ambiguity. Sin is not kept entirely away from the Christ of Schenkel, but just far enough away to prevent it from attaining such a development in him as in the Christ of Renan. Schenkel's Christ wavers unsteadily between the sinful Christ of Renan and the sinless Christ of the Church.

Schenkel has tried to make up for the lack of inner life in his development, by the coloring of his representation. Jesus is the man of the people, — who took an interest in the poor, oppressed people, who went about and taught and labored among the people, and for the people suffered and died. The men of the people are to him " the men of the Christian future." * His enemies are the "high-church party," " the theologues," — the stubborn bigots, the priesthood. His task is to do away with the law (again and again is this word repeated throughout the book), the artificial, empty, dead, creed-bound churchdom. His religion is that of humanity, — " the religion of the *love of man*, cleansed from the prejudices of religion and place,

---

* Schenkel's Char., S. 60 (Furness's Trans., vol. i. p. 136).

from all prepossessions, official and national," * the way of eternal life. The religious communion of the New Testament is to be founded, not upon official authority and scholasticism, not upon theology and clergy, not upon privileged orders, but upon the love of the people. Jesus thus proclaims the religion free from every ceremonial statute, proclaims the freedom of worship, proclaims human worth and human rights, proclaims the socialistic principle. By not excluding Judas from the last supper, he showed that all Church discipline is useless; he has not tied the communion to a definite preparation, or to a definite creed, but has granted to every one absolute freedom to partake of it. You perceive the Jesus of Schenkel expresses himself very decidedly about the questions of to-day: he is the genuine demagogue of the present, who, with his struggle against the law and against feudal prejudices, might come out with applause everywhere in behalf of free religion and the socialistic principle. But that is not the historical Jesus, the Jesus of the Gospels, the Jesus of Peter and Paul. He proclaimed neither free religion nor human rights: he did not proclaim any thing; for he did "not cry, nor lift up, nor cause his voice to be heard in the street."† It is true that he did not court the favor of the privileged classes; but it is also true that he did not, like Schenkel's Jesus, flatter the people without teaching them that every thing must be

---

* Schenkel's Char., S. 127 (Furness's Trans., vol. ii. p. 86).
† Isaiah xlii. 2 (Matthew xii. 19).

built up from below, from the good-will and pure disposition of the people. This portrait of Christ is really as unhistorical as Renan's. While Renan's "Life of Jesus" is a romance, Schenkel's "Character of Jesus" is a party-pamphlet, in which the enemies of the Lord are so drawn, that they look precisely like Schenkel's enemies, — that is, as he represents them to himself, — and in which words are put into the mouth of the Lord which plainly show that he is fighting directly for Schenkel and his party.

There is at present a kind of historical writing, which is fond of borrowing the colors for its pictures directly from the present time. The constitutional contests of the Roman republic are related as if writers were telling about the constitutional contests of yesterday. It may seem as if in this way history might be brought home to us, and made fruitful for the present. I am not of that opinion. This kind of historical composition lacks the chief thing, without which the history of the past cannot be the teacher of the present: it lacks the truth. Most decidedly must it be rejected, when the sacred history is so treated. If anybody wishes to write a party-pamphlet, let him write one; but he desecrates what is most holy when he misuses the life of Jesus in the service of party-warfare, in order to make a party-pamphlet out of that.

Such are the facts concerning one of the two predicates which Schenkel claims for his "Character of Jesus;" namely, "truly historical." Let us now see what the other is worth; namely, "genuinely human." It must first be asked what Schenkel means by this. "Genuinely human" the Church also believes her Christ to be; she has at all times laid as much stress upon this, that Christ is truly man, as upon the fact that he is truly God. But this doctrine of the two natures in Christ asserts what is utterly impossible, according to Schenkel. Such a twofold being, God and man in one, is inconceivable. If he is truly God, he cannot be truly man. It is plain that with Schenkel genuinely human means only human. With this idea he proceeds to describe Christ for us as a mere man. But although a mere man, wholly within the bounds of human nature, as Schenkel likes to express it, Jesus is nevertheless said to be the archetype of humanity, the light of the world, the only one who has revealed the ideal of godly life as perfectly as is possible within the bounds of human nature. Schenkel does not even hesitate to call him the only-begotten Son of God, and speaks of his divinity, which, to be sure, is said to be not an essential equality with God, but a moral oneness, a perfectly sinless agreement of his will with the will of the Father.

The question arises whether these two assertions are consistent with each other, — a mere man, and sinless. If Jesus was only a man, it is inexplicable how he, and he alone of all men, should be perfectly sinless. His life was wholly within the bounds of human nature; and yet is he said to be the single Example, the archetype, the light of the world? If he is only a man, he cannot be the single Example, the ideal that shall rule for ever. He may be a remarkable personage, to whom our race is much indebted: but he is one among others, there are others by his side; and if they are inferior to him in some respects, in other respects they surpass him. Thus, brought within the course of the development of our race, he may always mark one of its greatest eras, but not the absolute acme of human greatness. There can be no such person. We stand upon the ground of relativity; and it is a contradiction to say of any one, that he is only a man, and yet the single Example for all time, the light of the world. If Schenkel is decided that there is nothing supernatural in Jesus, nothing but a human nature, no capacity in him which does not belong to human nature in general, then he must cease to call him the single Example, the archetype, the light of the world. If he still does it, then either these high predicates are not seriously meant, or his portrait has no claim, according to his own premises, to be "genuinely human."

Let us, I pray you, look these things straight in the face. All equivocation must vanish here where the really decisive point is at stake,—the heart and centre of our faith. Schenkel says that we cannot have faith in the rationalistic Christ. He wishes, then, for a Christ in whom we can have faith; and his Christ is doubtless meant to be such a one. Let us see. We can have faith only in God. That is a simple but fundamental proposition; without holding it fast, Christianity ceases to be monotheistic, sinks below Mohammedanism, down to the grade of heathenism. It is also a proposition which the old rationalism maintained in its day without equivocation, and with a moral energy which might well be imitated at the present time. We are now obliged to confront the following alternative: Either the Christ of Schenkel is a mere man like other men, remarkable, perhaps the most remarkable of all, but only within the bounds of human nature, — and hence we dare not have faith in him; hence the want is not satisfied, the want which Schenkel himself feels, of a Christ in whom we can have faith: or we can have faith in him, — and hence he is not a mere man; and the task which Schenkel has undertaken of giving us a "genuinely human" Christ, is not performed.

No one has exposed the contradictions in which Schenkel has entangled himself more acutely than Strauss. With a consistency which leaves nothing to be desired, he has laid bare the ambiguity of Schenkel's position. In his view, Schenkel's sinless Christ is as great a miracle as the Church's Son of God, born of a virgin; and still more inconceivable, since the Church acts in general on the ground of the supernatural and miraculous, while Schenkel rejects this, and yet admits the miracle of a sinless Christ. He shows, with acute severity, the inconsistency of Schenkel's propositions. If the perfection of Christ is only such as is possible within the bounds of human nature, then such perfection must be possible for all who share in human nature; and, as always happens with other perfections of which human nature is capable, must, in some instances at least, have come to pass. The Church says absolute perfection is only possible for Christ, and therefore came to pass only in him; and this is clearly correct logic. Schenkel says relative perfection is possible for all men, but came to pass only in Christ, — which is as absurd as it would be to say, that perfection was only possible for Christ, but came to pass in other men.

There is no such ambiguity in Strauss. With him there is perfect consistency, which shrinks from no result; perfect candor, which scorns to conceal its aim. Strauss, without any reserve, proposes to destroy the illusion of miracles. The irrefragable part of Christianity is, that it has raised mankind above the sensuous religion of the Greeks, and above the legal religion of the Jews; but the faith that a spiritual, moral power rules the world, and the knowledge that the service of this power must be spiritual and moral, — all this, says Strauss, has not really amounted to any thing in Christianity up to this time. Even Protestantism still depends upon a number of external performances, which are no better than Jewish ceremonies. The cause of this is the illusion of miracles. As long as Christianity is regarded as something outwardly given, Christ as one who has come from heaven, the Church as an institution for expiation through his blood, — so long is the religion of the Spirit itself unspiritual; Christianity is a Jewish idea. The task of the present day is to destroy this illusion of miracles. This is also the only means of success for the agitation in behalf of a freer Church constitution, which Strauss looks down upon rather contemptuously. "He who would banish priests from the Church must first banish miracles from religion."*

Strauss is perfectly serious in this intention. No trace of accommodation can be found in him. Jesus is a man like other men; a remarkable person, who has rendered great service to mankind, by first expressing the ideas of the religion of the Spirit: but he is not the single Example,—the archetype. Strauss thinks that to say, as Schenkel says, Jesus is the light of the world, is dishonest flattery. Sinlessness, perfection, of course, cannot be attributed to him: that belongs to the supernatural illusion about Jesus. He had great gifts, but he also had his failings; he occupies an important place in history, but he had his predecessors, and he will have successors.

Strauss is equally consistent in his treatment of the authorities. He does not use the Gospel of John at one time as an unhistorical book, and at another as a good historical authority; he does not accept one story and reject the rest, nor separate in the same story an historical kernel from a legendary hull. Strauss is not given to such tricks. The

---

* Strauss's Leben Jesu (gearbeitet), S. xix. (Authorized Trans., vol. i. p. xvi.).

Gospel which he judges to be the earliest of all — the Gospel of Matthew — is merely a cloudy medium, obscured by the lapse of time, and by all sorts of intervening events. At the early day of its composition, much may have been already lost; many a significant word, many an act, of Jesus may have been forgotten. Much also may have been added; words which he did not speak, deeds which he did not do, events which did not take place.

The authorities, therefore, do not furnish materials for a sure, life-like picture of Jesus. "People do not like to hear it," — thus Strauss concludes his investigations, — " and therefore they do not believe it; but whoever has thoroughly studied the subject, and is candid, knows as well as we do, that history gives us concerning few great men such unsatisfactory information as concerning Jesus."[*] The figure of Socrates, for instance, four hundred years older, is incomparably more distinct. What Strauss gives as the life of Jesus is therefore extremely barren. He knows nothing certainly about him, except that he was born, that he taught, and that he died. What he taught can seldom be determined with certainty. The case is not so bad as has been asserted, — that it is impossible to learn that any one of the sayings attributed by the Gospels to Jesus were said by him. There are some which we

---

[*] Strauss's Leben Jesu (gearbeitet), S. 621. [This passage begins the second paragraph of the Conclusion of Strauss's work, and may probably be found at the end of vol. ii. of the Authorized Trans. — The translator has been unable to get that volume.]

may, in all probability, ascribe to Jesus; but this probability, approaching nearly to certainty, does not extend very far, and the case looks much worse for the acts and general occurrences of the life of Jesus, excepting his journey to Jerusalem. It is unnecessary to go into details. I could say little more than what has just been said. We must dispense entirely with details of the life of Jesus. For instance, from the account of the youth of Jesus, we know certainly only that he was born in Nazareth, that his father was probably a carpenter; and we may also suppose, that, in the names of his parents Joseph and Mary, there is a remnant of historical fact. The later periods of his life are furnished with like scantiness. Such events even as the solemn entry of Jesus into Jerusalem receive no quarter from Strauss's criticism. We are left again wholly in the dark.

We must in the first place acknowledge the candor of Strauss. He disdained to put into the empty place an image of his own make, a Christ of romance like Renan's, or a partisan Christ like Schenkel's. He simply left the place empty. We must content ourselves with not knowing who Christ was. One is involuntarily reminded of the saying of the man who was born blind (John ix. 30), "Why, herein is a marvellous thing, that ye know not from whence he is, and yet he hath opened mine eyes." A marvellous thing indeed! From this Jesus proceeds a movement which revolutionizes the world; and we know less about his life than we know about the life of Socrates, who also exerted an influence, to be sure, but in a comparatively temporary and narrow circle. If such a deep movement really proceeded from Jesus, he must have made an impression upon his disciples, and must have left this impression, the likeness of himself, in their memory. Can it be said, that, scarcely half a century afterwards, all traces of this portrait were lost, and an entirely different, essentially false one had taken its place? A still more wonderful thing remains. This Jesus preaches the pure religion of the spirit; his disciples,— in whom, as Strauss expresses it, a thick layer of Jewish prejudices prevented the pure conception of the Messianic idea — did not understand him at all; put something totally different in its place, an unspiritual, substantially Jewish religion: and this, nevertheless, conquers the world. Strauss cannot, if he would, do away with the fact, that not his Christ, but the Christ of the Gospels; not his Christianity, but the Christianity of the apostles,— conquered the world, and has ruled it up to this time. The disciples therefore, or whoever made the representations of Christ in the Gospels, are the founders of this Christianity, which, though it is not the true one of Strauss, is the world-conquering and world-governing Christianity. How did the disciples get the idea of this Christ? Very simply: by reasoning from the Old-Testament prophecies to their fulfilment in Jesus, by the constantly repeated argument,— this or that was prophesied of the Messiah and is expected of him, therefore he must have done it, spoken it, suffered it. This is the reasoning from which the idea of Christ in the Gospels, and with it all Christianity, arose. This, in the words of Lessing, is like hanging the world on the threads of a spider's web. The question now is, How did the disciples come to this conclusion? There must have been something to lead them to argue in this way. They could not have drawn this illogical conclusion out of nothing. If Jesus was no more, if he did no more than Strauss admits, if he made no greater impression, this conclusion is an utter impossibility.

Strauss shifts off the claim made in my first discourse that whoever denies the supernatural origin of Christianity must first prove its natural origin, by saying that this proof should not be demanded, because the extant authorities are not sufficient for it. Then we will modify our claim to this, that at least we shall not be asked to accept as history such evidently impossible and self-contradictory theories as these, — that the disciples, narrowed by Jewish prejudices, originated such a representation of Christ; and that the world-conquering movement of Christianity is based upon such an argument as that from the prophecy to the fulfilment.

How each one of these home-made pictures of Christ reflects the likeness of the man who made it! — a plain sign that it is merely his own fabrication. In Renan's Christ, we see the likeness of the ready, ingenious, sometimes charming, sometimes frivolous Frenchman; in Schenkel's Christ, we see the likeness of the ecclesiastical agitator; and, in Strauss's Christ, we see the likeness of the learned theorist, who builds the whole world on an inference.

All these things are substantially the same that Strauss discovered thirty years ago, and offered to the world. His standpoint remains the same, and his book is at bottom only a new edition of the earlier work. The development of criticism, during the last thirty years, has shown clearly enough that this was a failure.

We can hardly judge otherwise of Schenkel's book. In him the old rationalism has re-appeared. This is why Strauss attacks Schenkel so violently. It is his old enemy, rationalism, whom he fights in him. In no theologian of the present day are there so many characteristics of this as in Schenkel. He has the same doctrine of the accommodation of the Lord, the same natural explanation of miracles. For instance, in the treatment of the miracle at the wedding in Cana, or of the loaves and fishes, there is hardly any difference between him and the old Paulus of Heidelberg. His result is also substantially the same: Jesus is a wise teacher, who has freed us from the yoke of the law. He has, besides this, only put a new piece or two on the old garment, and given to the whole a somewhat different coloring, corresponding more to the present time. To this coloring belong a number of orthodox-sounding forms of speech, which are meant to be very differently understood. Schenkel speaks of miracles, but means a gift of nature; of the divinity

of Christ, but means only a moral agreement with
God; of an atonement for the sin of the world, but
means only that men have discovered that God will
not judge by the letter; of redemption, but means
only redemption from the law. Strip this all off,
give to Schenkel's words their true meaning, and
the Christ of Schenkel is, in all its principal features, the Christ of the old rationalism.

What does this imply? How can we explain this
falling-back to a standpoint long ago surmounted?
Schenkel desires, above all things, to influence the
people. In him the theologian is ruled entirely by
the ecclesiastical party-leader. Since he began to
be that, he has essentially modified his theology.
Schenkel's effort is, not to found a new theological
school, but a Church with a new constitution and a
new creed. For this he needs the people, and not
that part of it (which is altogether only a small
fragment) that is utterly indifferent to the Church
and Christianity, that would rather dispense with
them entirely; but the part which, while not agree-
ing with the old creed, still wishes to have a Church,
still wishes to celebrate Christmas and Easter, and
does not like to dispense with Sunday, with baptism,
and the Lord's Supper. In this part of our people,
the force of the old rationalism is still dominant.
The people do not understand the pantheism of
Strauss, or his ideal Christ, and would shrink in
horror from his radicalism. They understand only
the old rationalism; and a natural instinct has drawn
Schenkel thither. The whole movement of late

years, which has had Schenkel for its party-leader, is nothing but a re-action of the still surviving force of the old rationalism against the mightily growing strength of the faith. Schenkel, in his "Character of Jesus," has tried to draw for this tendency its Christ; and it is not surprising that the portrait bears the features of the Christ of the old rationalism.

Here lies the danger of the book. The work of Strauss I regard, at this moment, as less dangerous. According to its title, it is written for the people; but the people will not understand it, and therefore will not read it. Schenkel's book, also, is far from being written in a popular style; but his Christ has an affinity with the tendency which still sways a large part of our people. There is nevertheless a consolation. You cannot bring a dead man to life again, though you deck him with ever so many spangles, and thrust him with great bombast upon the stage. Such ambiguity as Schenkel's can gain much influence for a time, but never for a long time. The advancing controversy sets it aside; and the decision, long delayed, then comes so much the quicker. There is no need of very sharp eyes to see that Schenkel's Christ will not live long. Many at the present day, and many, as I believe, of honest hearts, give themselves up to the hope that they have found here an accommodation between the old faith and the ideas of the nineteenth century, and rejoice that they still remain Christians; but it will be shown soon enough that what they thought accommodation was merely an ambiguity, which withstood no serious attack. The fight, waxing hotter, will force decision, and will soon leave no other choice than either, with Strauss, to do away altogether with the so-called illusion of miracles, to set aside every thing supernatural in Christianity, and with it Christianity itself; or, with the Fathers, to stand by the old Christ, whom we do not first have to seek for, whom the Church has always had, and, thank God, still has.

I have endeavored to set before you the chief modern representations of the life of Jesus. My task, however, is not yet finished. The judgment concerning the view of the Church on the one hand, and these modern representations on the other, depends especially upon two questions, which we have already been obliged to touch upon in various ways. The first question is, Have we in the writings of the New Testament, particularly in the Gospels, really sure and sufficient historical authorities for the life of Jesus? The next question is concerning miracles, Are there miracles, or not? I propose to discuss these questions in two more discourses.

THIRD DISCOURSE.

THE GOSPELS.

AT the close of the preceding discourse, I remarked that there were two principal questions, upon which depended the judgment concerning the modern representations of Jesus on the one hand, and, to put it briefly, concerning the Church's view on the other hand. The first question related to the authorities: Have we in the writings of the New Testament, particularly in the Gospels, really trustworthy historical authorities for the life of Jesus? The next question related to miracles: Are there miracles, or not? The modern representations of the life of Jesus are based upon negative answers to both these questions: the view of the Church presupposes affirmative answers to both of them. It is true, each question is involved in the other. The following is among the chief reasons urged against our Gospels as trustworthy authorities: They relate incredible things; things which could not have taken place,—miracles. Then, again, when we appeal to the Gospels to prove the actual occurrence of miracles, our appeal is rejected, with the assertion, that the Gospels do not contain pure history, but merely a mixture of history and more or less legend and fiction; legendary, embellished history. I must, therefore, ask you beforehand to permit me, not only to distinguish the first question from the second, but also to keep the two questions entirely separate; otherwise, an unbiassed examination of the first question is impossible. If any one approaches the Gospels with the presumption that no miracle is possible, their sentence is already pronounced; for they are full of miraculous stories, and further investigation is superfluous. The question whether miracles have occurred, and can occur, shall occupy us, God willing, at our next meeting: to-day, therefore, let us leave this entirely out of view, and examine (this question always excepted) the authorities for the history of Jesus, as impartially as a biographer, before he writes the life of any one, examines the authorities from which he must draw.

The only sources of information about the life of Jesus are the writings of the New Testament. Interesting as it would be to know what Jewish and Gentile contemporaries may have told about him and may have thought of him, that is impossible. What we have is insignificant and worthless. One passage of the Jewish historian Josephus, who lived at the time of the destruction of Jerusalem, and commanded a troop in the Jewish war against the Romans, is so uncertain in its text, that it thereby loses its value. What is furnished by Jewish tradition is of uncertain age, and is too much colored by hatred of Jesus to deserve further attention. Now and then, to be sure, bookselling industry brings to market such books as " Jesus the Essene," " Letters of an Essene concerning Jesus," and the like, which pretend to contain contemporaneous accounts concerning Jesus : this is mere imposture. The Gentiles are the same as silent; whenever they speak, they tell what they have learned from Christians : there remain for us only the writings of the New Testament. Before we begin to examine them, it may be well to premise some remarks of a general character, in order to get a view at the outset of what we have to expect.

We ask first, Are we, on the whole, upon ground where we may expect true history ? The answer is, Yes : we stand in a perfectly historical period, whose life is, in general, as clear and transparent to us as any period of antiquity can be. It is important to bring this home to our minds, for the case would be very different if the origin of Christianity fell in an age which could not pretend to established history. The facts of the origin of Christianity did not happen in secret or in a corner, but took place in the open day, before the eyes of a whole people, whose own magistrates, the supreme council and the Roman governor, were concerned in them.

We ask next, Was there an interest in this history among the circles of the primitive Christians, — an interest to explore it, and to transmit it safely ?

It must be answered, Yes, in the highest degree. The preaching of the gospel was at the start the relation of history: it had to be so. When the apostles went forth preaching Jesus is the Christ, no one knew who this Christ was; therefore they were obliged to begin by telling their hearers the history of Jesus. Without relating history, they could not advance a step. So essential was the historical account to the growth of the Church, that Paul mentions, among the offices with which the Church was furnished, an office of evangelists. The history of Jesus, the history of his work, is intrinsically the object of the Christian faith. Christianity is not a system of doctrine, which one can propound without imparting any thing concerning him who established it: it is history. Never has any religious communion had a greater interest in the history of its founder than the Christian Church. How different are the relations of Mohammedanism to its founder! and yet active exertions are now being made to establish securely the tradition concerning Mohammed and the founding of Islam. We cannot suppose that the oldest Church should not also have done what it could in this respect. It is hard to believe that it carelessly permitted legend to be substituted for history: there are sure signs also to the contrary. I will mention only a single instance, — the carefulness with which Paul, in the First Epistle to the Corinthians, specifies the witnesses of the resurrection. We should by no means suppose that he only preached Christ is risen! Upon this statement he would have received as little credit at that day, as any one would receive at the present time, who should say that So-and-so has risen from the dead. He brought witnesses who had seen the risen Christ to corroborate his own testimony. It has been said, in order to make the whole ground insecure from beginning to end, that that age made no use, in Christian circles at least, of criticism; that it was wholly uncritical; that, consequently, a reliable judgment concerning what are and what are not trustworthy authorities is not to be expected from it. That age certainly did know little of what is now called criticism: instead of it, it possessed in a high degree what was then, as now, the chief thing in all criticism, — appreciation of the truth. Besides, since the history in question was such as to involve the hatred of the whole world when it was professed, and might lead to disgrace and even to death, people were apt to inquire carefully beforehand upon what ground it rested. Every thing is opposed to the view, that the Church acted so uncritically as to accept any thing that seemed edifying, without regard for its truth. Tertullian incidentally speaks of a presbyter who forged a history about Paul and Thekla, and published it as true. When this was discovered, he was punished by removal from office. That does not agree very well with the assertion, that the age was wholly uncritical. The Church used actual criticism upon the Gospels, since it selected our four Gospels from a number of others.

But I will not begin with the Gospels: that ground is too disputed to start from. Let us start from ground that is entirely undisputed,—from the four Epistles of Paul, which the most extreme criticism has been obliged to let stand. These are the Epistle to the Romans, the two Epistles to the Corinthians, and the Epistle to the Galatians. That they are genuine writings, really composed by the Apostle Paul, is established beyond the possibility of a doubt. Let us see what they contain concerning the history of Jesus.

It may, perhaps, appear strange that there is so little of this. The apostle seldom relates any thing about Jesus, and seldom quotes a word from him. Reflection, however, makes the explanation easy. The Epistles were not written to interest Jews or Gentiles in Christ for the first time, but to guide and to strengthen in their faith those who had been previously won. It is evident to the careful reader, that Paul always presupposes an historical foundation: the life of Jesus is known to his readers; a detailed historical account has clearly gone before. Paul refers to this only when it is necessary. How often he alludes to what he has already told them, — to "his gospel" (Rom. ii. 16)! When there is occasion for it, some particular is mentioned, something is occasionally given in detail,—such as the institution of the Lord's Supper, and the account of the resurrection.

By collecting what the Epistles give in this way, we get the chief facts of the life of Jesus,—his descent from the family of David (Rom. i. 3); his birth from a woman (1 Cor. xi. 23, *et seq.*); his crucifixion, death, burial, and resurrection (1 Cor. xv. 1, *et seq.*). We can infer still more with perfect certainty. The way in which Paul speaks of baptism (Rom. vi. 4; 1 Cor. xii. 13; 1 Cor. i. 17; Gal. iii. 27, *et al.*) certainly leads us to the inference, that he recognized it as established by Christ; and when he traces to the Lord the miraculous power of the apostles (1 Cor. xii., *et al.*), he must regard Christ as the most original and the richest possessor of this power. Paul gives few details, for the reason just stated; but those which he gives agree entirely with the evangelical accounts, — for instance, that the rulers of Israel were guilty of Jesus' death (1 Cor. ii. 8); that he was betrayed (1 Cor. xi. 23); that he rose again the third day (1 Cor. xv. 4). Paul's whole representation of Jesus is precisely the same as that of the Gospels. Jesus, in his view, is not merely the sinless, holy man (1 Cor. xv. 21; Rom. v. 19): he is more than man, — he is the Son of God (Rom. i. 4; Gal. iv. 4, *et al.*) and the son of David, who was rich in divine glory, and for our sakes became poor (2 Cor. viii. 9); he is the mediator in the creation of the world (1 Cor. viii. 6); the man from heaven (1 Cor. xv. 47), who now sits at the right hand of God (Rom. viii. 34), and shall come back from heaven to judge the world (Rom. ii. 16); he is Lord in the highest sense, the object and substance of faith and of worship. We need only read these four Epistles of Paul to become convinced that the Christ of Paul was a different person from him whom Renan, Strauss, and Schenkel now offer us as the truly historical Christ.

Paul was not the only individual who believed in this Christ. Add to his Epistles the first Epistle of Peter, which all sober criticism must admit to be a genuine Epistle of this apostle. Here also is the same idea of Christ. Take the Revelation of John, which, according to modern criticism, passes for a genuine writing of the apostle. Whether it is really his, or is the work of another John (opinions still differ about it), at all events it is a writing of the apostolic age, and it gives no other idea of Christ. In it he is the First and the Living One, the Alpha and the Omega (Rev. i. 8, 11, *et al.*), the object of divine veneration and worship (Rev. i. 17, *et al.*). The Church can comfort herself, therefore, with the assurance that her own idea of Christ is that of the apostolic age,—is that of Peter and Paul, and of the apostolic man who wrote the Apocalypse.

If this idea is said to be false, consider what the assertion means. It means no less than that the apostolic age,—that the very persons, part of whom were eye-witnesses, part of whom were acquainted with eye-witnesses, formed for themselves a false idea of the Lord. If it is said that the Church afterwards erroneously deified the man Jesus, and this is the error from which Christianity must be freed, in order to recover its original purity, we reply that this pretended error at least began very soon, so soon, that pure Christianity — pure according to such notions of purity — never existed. Any one is at liberty, of course, to discard the idea of Christ given by Peter and Paul; but then let him be honest enough to say so: he can put another representation in its place, and then let him not act as if he could summon the apostolic age as evidence in its favor, but openly say that this portrait of Christ is of his own make. If we had not a single line more from the apostolic age than the writings just cited, these documents alone would be sufficient to enable us to say with perfect certainty, the Christ of Renan, of Strauss, and of Schenkel, is not the truly historical Christ.

As we now turn to the Gospels, we must think of their origin as simply and naturally as possible. It is true that over all and in all rules the Holy Spirit, whose task, as the Lord expressly indicated, was to remind his disciples of all that he had said unto them, taking care that the future Church should not lack a sure, sufficient likeness of her Founder and Head for her faith and life. The way of the Spirit, however, is not to suppress what is natural, but to purify it; and it is with this human, natural side of the formation of the Gospels that we have now to deal. It is self-evident that not the written record, but the oral tradition, of the acts and speeches of the Lord came first; especially since the thoughts and hopes of the primitive Christians were not directed towards a distant future of the Church upon earth, but towards a speedy second-coming of the Lord. The written record is only the final, most perfect account of this oral tradition.

At first every eye-witness and ear-witness related what he had seen or heard; and while the apostles, who had accompanied Jesus during his whole public ministry, were thereby able to give the fullest and most correct information concerning his life, they were of course followed by others, who collected, in addition to what they had themselves seen, reports from other witnesses. Groups and series of stories about the Lord and his discourses were formed. People took pleasure in telling and hearing as much as possible of what the Lord said and did; but they did not undertake to collect all of his words, or to recount all of his miracles. The entire history which we possess is only a selection; and this selection was, humanly speaking, influenced by all sorts of accidental circumstances. People from Galilee must have gladly and often told stories of the Galilean ministry of the Lord; and, since the majority of his first followers were Galileans, the Galilean stories formed the largest part of the oral tradition, from the beginning to the end. When some one who had been healed by the Lord became afterwards an active member of the Church, an especial interest was then attached to the story of this cure; for they had the living witness there with them. It is probable, for instance, that we owe to some such circumstance the mention of the name of the blind Bartimæus, the son of Timæus (Mark x. 46); or the mention of Simon the Cyrenian, the father of Alexander and Rufus (Mark xv. 21). Bartimæus, Alexander, and Rufus were known as members of the Church; and the story was naturally told with the familiar names. In other cases the names were soon lost, as in every popular tale; and the story was told merely of a leper or a paralytic, without any names. The same thing happened with accounts of times and places. There was no special interest in these at first. The main point was, that the Lord had healed this or that sick person, had spoken this or that word; and it was not very important when and where he had done it. These oral traditions concerning the life of the Lord should not, therefore, be thought of as a complete biography, with every fact and date correctly arranged; although the chief points, his death and his resurrection, must have been contained in every account.

The desire must have early arisen to commit to writing what had been orally transmitted. A record of what had been heard was important for one's self, and useful as a means of enlightening foreign brethren who asked for information. The first records naturally originated in this way. These did not comprehend every thing, but were simple transcripts of the oral tradition. The wider the Church spread, the farther time advanced, the greater the interest in written records necessarily became; and, apart from other evidence, the introduction to the

Gospel of Luke shows plainly enough that there were a great number of writings besides our Gospels, which related more or less correctly the life and ministry of the Lord. Our first three Gospels form the most complete result of this process, and have therefore been acknowledged by the Church.

These must be first considered apart from the fourth Gospel. The fourth Gospel stands entirely alone; for, as we see at a glance, it gives much that is different, recounts different miracles, repeats different discourses, from the first three Gospels. These three, as no one who has read them can fail to observe, are most intimately connected with one another. They not only tell substantially the same story, but they frequently agree in the style of narration, and in the very words. They are so much alike, that we have their accounts put side by side, as parallels. This combination is called "synopsis," a word derived from the Greek; and hence the first three Gospels are called Synoptic Gospels. The explanation of their relationship is one of the hardest problems of New-Testament science. Serious attempts to solve this problem were first undertaken about the beginning of this century. Numerous theories have been advanced, and some one of them has always routed the others; but it would lead us too far to consider them at present. I will only add, that formerly the inclination was towards regarding the Gospel of Mark as the latest, and as an abstract from the other two; but lately— especially since Ewald's works on the question, which have justly received manifold acknowledgment — the views more and more unite in the contrary direction, towards holding the Gospel of Mark as the earliest, and as the basis of the other two. Nevertheless, this whole problem should not be thought to be at all certainly solved. There are still not a few scholars of the most opposite tendencies who hold and defend other views.

This whole inquiry is not so important for us as the question, *When* did our Gospels originate? The judgment concerning their trustworthiness depends mainly upon this. The nearer they are to the events which they relate, the more surely may we expect trustworthy evidence in them; on the other hand, the farther their origin is removed from the apostolic age, the more possible, at least, is it that legend had crept into them. The Tübingen school therefore sought to bring down the Gospels as far as possible into the second century. According to Baur, the Gospel of Matthew was first written between 130 and 134; that of Luke, not before 150. But we certainly find the Synoptic Gospels in the common and acknowledged use of the Church as early as 140–150. As early as the middle of the second century, a heathen enemy of Christianity, Celsus, quotes from them his information about the person and the work of Jesus, as from books that were generally known. We find them still earlier, 130–140, among the Gnostic heretics. One of these, Marcion, worked over the Gospel of Luke for his own purposes, — an irrefragable proof that this Gospel was then widely known. Therefore it cannot be doubted that the Gospels must have originated some time before this. Accordingly, a backward movement began in the Tübingen school itself. Baur's disciples set the Gospels farther and farther back. Zeller thinks Luke was written about 130; Volckmar puts Mark about 80, Luke 100, Matthew 110; Köstlin puts the original draught of Matthew between 70 and 80, its elaboration in its present form 90–100, Luke a little earlier, Mark a little later; Hilgenfeld puts Matthew and Mark about the end of the first century, Luke in the beginning of the second century. This brings us substantially into the first century; and now Ewald, and the latest investigators of the subject, Weiss and Holtzmann, go still farther back. According to Ewald, Mark wrote after Peter's death; the Gospel of Matthew originated before the destruction of Jerusalem, consequently before 70; the Gospel of Luke five or ten years after the end of the Jewish war, consequently 75–80. Similar results are reached by Holtzmann, who also places the older authorities, upon which our Synoptic Gospels are originally based, with these Gospels within the years 60–80.

Sober scientific study, whose conclusions are not foregone, can reach no other results. The external evidence alone, apart from all other, does not permit it. This is as good and as sure as we could desire from an age in which little was written, and from which less has come down to us. All that we have from the period between the end of the apostolic age and the middle of the second century, could be comprised in a medium-sized volume; and yet there is no lack of evidence for all three Gospels.

To begin with Mark. The oldest tradition testifies unanimously that he composed his Gospel under the special influence of Peter, whose interpreter he was. Papias,* for instance, a man whose life extends into the apostolic age, cites a still more ancient witness, — John the Presbyter, — and says, "Mark, the interpreter of Peter, wrote down accurately what he remembered of Peter's discourses about the words and works of the Lord." Yes: Christian antiquity goes in many ways so far back, as to treat Mark's Gospel as a Gospel of Peter. According to external and internal arguments, it cannot have been written later than about 65.

The Gospel of Luke has its surest evidence in the Acts. There can be no doubt, that these two writings, making as they do one whole, are the work of a single author. The author of the Book of Acts appears in it as a travelling companion of Paul; and, although he nowhere mentions his own name, antiquity testifies unanimously that he was Luke. This agrees with the thoroughly Pauline tone of the Gospel of Luke. According to many signs, this Gospel was first written after the destruction of Jerusalem.

The Gospel of Matthew is in a somewhat different condition. According to the tradition of the Church,†

---

* See Note I. p. 152. † See Note II. p. 153.

Matthew wrote originally not Greek, but Hebrew, — or, to speak more accurately, Aramaic, the popular language of his time. This Aramaic composition of the apostle most probably did not comprise all of our present first Gospel, but was a collection of the Lord's discourses, accompanied perhaps with bits of narrative. This collection was then enlarged to a complete Gospel, and in this form was translated into Greek. As for the time of its composition, the collection of discourses must have been made very early; for the Gospel itself in its Greek translation, according to external and internal evidence, must be placed within the sixty years preceding the destruction of Jerusalem.

We find, on summing up the results, that our Synoptic Gospels were written in the apostolic age, — to mark the time only very generally, between 60 and 75; and although no one of them, as we possess it, is the work of an immediate disciple of Jesus, they still point indirectly to such persons, — the first to Matthew, the second to Peter.

Let us notice what must follow from these considerations.

When any one asserts that our Gospels contain, not history, but legend, or at least history transformed and embellished by legend, he must be able to prove the possibility of such a comprehensive legendary formation. Every legendary growth requires, to speak of nothing else, a certain time. When the true idea of an historical personage is obscured by distance of time, and there remains only a general impression of its character, then the growth of legend first becomes possible to any great degree. Where is there time for such a thing in this case? There are only about thirty years between the Lord's death and the composition of Mark. A large number of persons who had seen the Lord, who had themselves gone through this history, were still living. Paul was able to appeal to hundreds of eye-witnesses of the resurrection. Is there room here for much of a legendary growth? Remember what I have previously remarked, that we are standing in a perfectly historical age. The character of the age was far more that of unbelief than of naïve belief. Such an age can intentionally create religious fiction, or all kinds of fantastic figures of superstition, which at that time, as always, went side by side with unbelief; but it is not inclined to a naïve formation of legend. And what attitude did the apostles take towards this legendary growth, which not only began in their day, but must have then displayed its greatest activity? It is inconceivable that the apostles, with their moral purity and thoroughly sincere characters, took part in this; or that they repeated to the Church as history these legends which had grown up without their aid. If we cannot suppose this, how can we fancy that these legends, without the aid of the apostles, or in spite of their direct contradiction, found acceptance and belief in the churches, which were wont in every particular to look up to the apostles as the witnesses appointed by the Lord?

Finally, I pray you to notice another point. If the disciples, the eye-witnesses and ear-witnesses, received only a moderately deep impression of Jesus; if they preserved only a moderately correct idea of him as he lived among them,—it cannot be thought possible, that, during the thirty or forty years which intervened between the death of the Lord and the composition of our Gospels, an unhistorical and legendary idea of Christ should have intruded itself into the place of the genuine historical idea. Whoever asserts that the gospel picture of Christ is not truly historical, must make up his mind to say that the disciples got no true idea of the Lord from their intercourse with him, so that a false conception could easily foist itself upon them; or, in other words, he must make up his mind to say, that the person, the words, and the works of Jesus made no real impression. Then let him explain how it comes to pass, that the whole great movement of the world represents itself as proceeding from the person of Jesus. If any thing is settled, this is settled: that Jesus made an impression upon his contemporaries, of a depth, a liveliness, and a permanency, such as no one else ever made. Hence, during the thirty or forty years after his death, they who had been his companions must have had a lively, genuine, and true idea of him; and if we suppose that only the essential contents of the Synoptic Gospels originated during this period,—which according to the present position of science may be considered certain,—the picture of Christ which they give us must be this genuine, historical idea.

In the fourth Gospel, we have evidence which is still more direct. If this was written by John, it gives us an account of the life of Jesus, than which there could be no better, — the account of one of his own disciples, of his most intimate disciple. The importance of the question of the genuineness of John's Gospel has been recognized on all sides; and the discussions concerning it have been so active during late years, that their literature alone would make a small library. I am therefore the more sensible of the difficulty of giving you even an approximately adequate representation of it. In order to do this, it will be necessary to go into many details, although the limits of a discourse oblige a restriction to the main points.

The first question concerns the external evidence for the fourth Gospel. Who knows it, and vouches for its Johannine origin?

Let us start from that point of time when it was generally acknowledged and used in the Church as an apostolic writing. This was about 180. At this time, Irenæus used it in Lyons; and the Church in that place cited it in a letter which it wrote on the occasion of the great persecution of 177. It is also found in use in the Roman Church, as an old scriptural index of this Church proves; and by the Alexandrian and Syrian Churches, as is proved by the writings of Clement of Alexandria for the one, and by the Syrian translation of the Bible for the other. There is no contradiction of this: only a small sect, the so-called Alogi, rejected it, solely because it did not agree with them. If there had been at that time the slightest recollection of a later origin of this Gospel, they would certainly have taken advantage of it; but there is no trace of such a thing. This Gospel belongs to the undisputed, generally acknowledged Scriptures.

The testimony of Irenæus, just mentioned, is especially important. He had formerly lived in Asia Minor, and was a disciple of Polycarp of Smyrna, who had personally known John. Irenæus's testimony,[*] therefore, points directly into the circle in which the Gospel originated. Can we suppose that Irenæus would have accepted a Gospel as coming from John, if he had never heard of such a Gospel from the men who lived with John?

We can go still farther back. The next witness we meet is Justin Martyr, a number of whose writings, from the years 138–160, are in our possession. Justin did not yet have the separate selection of our four Gospels, but used also several which were afterwards not acknowledged by the Church. He calls them altogether, " Memoirs of the Apostles." Among them was certainly the Gospel of John. He quotes several passages which are to be found in this alone ; and, what is more important, there are many Johannine expressions in his own style, and his whole method of teaching can be understood only by supposing him to have been familiar with John's Gospel.

This evidence has been further corroborated by a

[*] See Note III. p. 154.

remarkable discovery of late years. It was asked by our opponents, If Justin possessed the fourth Gospel, why did he not use it oftener? Its rare use was said to make it doubtful that it had been used at all. Then there appeared a precisely similar case in another writing of the period, — the so-called "Clementine Homilies," a Christian romance which originated in heretical circles probably about 150–160, but which we did not possess entire, for the end of the manuscript was wanting. A complete manuscript was found in a Roman library; and, lo! one of the last chapters contained, word for word, the whole story of the man that was born blind, from John ix. Thereby we not only gain indubitable evidence for the date about 160, but also the testimony of Justin is corroborated. Volckmar, to be sure, reverses the matter, and asserts that the author of the fourth Gospel made use of Justin, — a plainly desperate shift. Hilgenfeld, on the contrary, went back a step. Baur still thought the Gospel originated about 150, but Hilgenfeld put it back into the years 120–140.

Let us now go farther back, and explore the period before 150. This also has been illuminated by a new discovery.* A few years ago, in Paris, a manuscript was found, before unnoticed, which on closer examination proved to be a writing of the celebrated ancient bishop, Hippolytus, "Against all Heresies." This contains accurate accounts of many Gnostic sects of the time, and, what is espe-

* See Note IV. p. 154.

cially important, many extracts from their lost writings. Here we learn that the leaders of the Gnostic party, Basilides and Valentine, used the Gospel of John as early as 130–140. When we consider how slowly books spread in those days, we may certainly say, that if this Gospel was used by the Gnostics as early as 130–140, — they merely appropriating what they found already acknowledged by the Church, — then it must have originated at the latest about 110–120.

To this period Schenkel goes back. Whoever is obliged to date the writing of the fourth Gospel so early as this, is utterly unable to assume that it is entirely unauthentic; and Schenkel consequently does not assume that. When we remember, that, according to all witnesses, John lived until the beginning of the second century, we could perhaps understand how a Gospel could have been fathered upon him about 140–150; but that this happened about ten years after his death, and that such a Gospel should have been accepted without hesitation as genuine, — this cannot be understood.

But we have witnesses who reach still farther back. Their testimony is indirect, but not the less important on that account. Papias and Polycarp are acquainted with the First Epistle of John. Polycarp quotes a passage from it. The author of the First Epistle is certainly the author of the Gospel. Thus we have the testimony, though indirect, of a man who had associated with John. Many ways of escape from this decisive testimony have been tried, but all the trials are in vain. It has been denied, that the Gospel and the Epistle were by the same author. Baur declares the Epistle to be a weak imitation of the Gospel. Hilgenfeld reverses their relation, and puts the Epistle first. In my opinion, whoever once reads, without prejudice, the Epistle and the Gospel, will no longer deny that one man must have written both. It has been said that the occurrence of single sentences does not prove that the whole Epistle was yet in existence. This means that there is nothing to say. It has been denied that the Epistle of Polycarp himself is genuine. This is mere violence. For the Epistle of Polycarp, we have the certain testimony of Irenæus, his disciple. Here the various evidence concentrates. Irenæus, who personally knew Polycarp, testifies that he wrote the Epistle which bears his name. In this Epistle, Polycarp, who personally knew John, quotes his first Epistle. If the Epistle is Johannine, so must the Gospel be. I do not see how this evidence can be broken.

The result of our investigation must be the acknowledgment, that there is no want of external evidence for the Gospel; that it is as well authenticated as any other writing of the New Testament.*

The opponents of its genuineness consequently lay more stress upon internal evidence. Formerly it was thought that no other Gospel bore so plainly the stamp of apostolic origin as this " tender, chief

---

* See Note V. p. 154.

Gospel;" but now it is said that the contents of this Gospel clearly betray the fact, that it could not have been written by John.

To begin with the most external part. A list of geographical and historical errors are given, as signs that the author was not accurately acquainted with the times and places in which the life of Jesus was spent, and therefore could not have been John. Schenkel even denies that he was an inhabitant of Palestine, and a Jew. Schenkel and Strauss cite four or five such errors. Even these opponents can find no more. Then the case must stand very well for John. Consider a moment. Some one, who is neither an inhabitant of Palestine nor a Jew, writes in the second century a life of Jesus, with accurate references to times and places, with the most detailed descriptions (in this very thing the fourth Gospel abounds more than any other); and in it the sharpest critical eyes can find no more than four or five errors in geography and history. This would be very wonderful; and therefore I think it may be said in general, before going farther, that the case looks very well for John. But even the supposed errors can by no means be certainly proved to be such. Let us examine those which are held to be the surest. According to chap. i. 28, John baptized in Bethany, on the farther side of the Jordan. The text is uncertain: many read, as our German Bible has it, Bethabara. Suppose we take Bethany as the correct reading. Then, it is said, the author of the fourth Gospel did not know where

Bethany lay: he thought it was on the farther side of the Jordan. Indeed! But we see elsewhere that he knew very well that Bethany lay in the neighborhood of Jerusalem. Did he, therefore, think that Jerusalem was also on the farther side of the Jordan? That is utterly inconceivable. Baur therefore supposes that he invented a second Bethany. This is improbable; for on the ground that the author was not John, and wished to pass for John, he would have kept as strictly as possible within the real localities. The simplest solution is to suppose that there were two places of the same name. Origen says there is no Bethany on the farther side of the Jordan; but such great changes had taken place in the land of the Jews during the two hundred and fifty years before Origen, that one of these places might have entirely disappeared: for nothing necessitates the theory of a great town, or even a village; and we know that John the Baptist rather avoided the larger places. Another error is said to be found in the conversation of Jesus with the Samaritan woman. The place in whose vicinity Jacob's well lay is called Sychar by the evangelist, whereas its name is given elsewhere as Sychem. Of this he is again supposed to be ignorant. But he describes the place exactly in other respects. The well lay near the town, according to his account; but Sychem, the present Nablus, is more than half a league distant from the well. Consequently this cannot be the place indicated; and there is not the least improbability in supposing that there was another place in the vicinity named Sychar.

It is about the same with the historical errors. It is said that the evangelist represents the relations between the Jews and Samaritans as far too hostile. The Jewish tradition in the Talmud describes it as still more hostile. The evangelist is said to have thought that the Jewish high-priest was chosen every year, like the Roman consuls; for he says of Caiaphas, "being high-priest that year." That would certainly be a great error, — so great that it can hardly, or rather cannot, be understood of one so well versed in the Old Testament as the evangelist evidently is, and who makes such frequent use of it. The phrase "being high-priest that year," is explained by the consideration, that John uses it when he speaks of the malevolent prophecy of Caiaphas. He thereby calls attention to the fact, that Caiaphas was high-priest that very year, — the memorable year of the Lord's death.

All of these pretended errors are found only because they are sought for.

No more valid is the objection, that the character of the Gospel does not agree with the character of John as we meet him elsewhere. It is said that the "son of thunder," as he is called in the Gospel of Mark, could not have written this Epistle and this Gospel, in which love alone is preached; and that the large-heartedness, which appears in the fourth Gospel free from all Judaism, is inconsistent with the narrow-minded Judaism of John. It is true that John was a son of thunder; but cannot a son of thunder become, by the power of grace, a disciple and preacher of love? At all events, the Church of Asia Minor has preserved such a recollection of John, which is shown by the familiar story, that, in his very old age, John used to say to the people in the Church nothing but the constantly repeated counsel, "Little children, love one another." The idea that he was a bigoted Judaist is a mere fancy of the Tübingen school, which also pretends that at Ephesus he destroyed the fruits of Paul's previous ministry. That is another thing which the memory of the Church of Asia Minor has not preserved. This Church regards the two Apostles Paul and John as its pillars, and has no misgivings of any opposition between them.

We now come to the chief of all the objections that are urged against the genuineness of the Gospel, that upon which our opponents lay the most stress, and which, if it were valid, would alone suffice to prove that the Gospel was not genuine. It is said that the fourth Gospel gives an entirely different representation of Christ from the first three; and so surely as theirs is true, this is false. One can but wish that they who argue in this way would first admit the picture of Christ given in the first three Gospels to be truly historical: I am sure that they would then come soon enough to the acknowledgment of the fourth Gospel.

A simple comparison only is needed to see, that the fourth Gospel, while coinciding in many parts with the first three, contains also much that is peculiar to itself; recounts miracles, repeats discourses of the Lord, which are not in the other Gospels. This, as it seems to me, is one of the strongest proofs of its genuineness; for an eye-witness speaks here who can adduce a deal of new material from his own recollection. Let us reverse the question, and ask, If it is not an eye-witness who speaks, but some unknown person of the second century, whence did this person get the abundant material? From oral tradition? This was very scanty as early as the beginning of the second century. From the growth of legend? Where in the second century is there the slightest trace that legend formed such stories as the marriage at Cana and the raising of Lazarus? There remains nothing else to be said, except — he invented it all. Baur did not hesitate to assert this, and Strauss agreed with him. They suppose that the author of the fourth Gospel spun these peculiar tales of his out of the Synoptic Gospels, and perhaps some other sources of information. For instance, he read in the parable of the rich man and poor Lazarus, that the rich man begged that Lazarus should be sent back to the earth, to preach repentance to his brethren. This suggested to him the idea of making Lazarus actually come back out of the grave. With this he united Luke's story of the two sisters of Bethany, made Lazarus the brother of Martha and Mary, and thus formed the narrative of the raising of Lazarus. That is indeed fine-spun. I do not know which we should most wonder at, — the fertility of the pseudo-John, who makes such a narrative out of single bits of information; or the penetration of the critics, who now, after eighteen hundred years, can find the traces of the origin of this narrative; or, finally, the credulity of those who believe this to be possible.

The author who had the ability to write such a Gospel as a fictitious narrative must certainly have been a very remarkable man. Who is there in the whole second century that even remotely approximates to him; that can be mentioned in the same breath with him? Search the second century through and through, and how far, how infinitely far, does every thing stand below this! The writings of Justin, or whatever else that is excellent in our inheritance from this period; the beautiful letter to Diognetus, a pearl of the ancient Christian literature,—there is still a deep gulf which separates them all from the fourth Gospel. Indeed, it may be said that all the difficulties which have been placed, with care and ingenuity, in the way of the genuineness, are as nothing in comparison with the difficulties over which one stumbles who denies the genuineness, and is obliged to bring down the fourth Gospel into the second century, and assign a place for it there; for it must have originated at some time. In this connection it will suffice to quote the opinion of a man who will be admitted to be impartial,— Professor Ritschl, of Göttingen. He declares that he holds this Gospel to be genuine with the rest, for this reason, " because the denial of its genuineness involves much greater difficulties than the acknowledgment of it."

Add to this the direct impression which the Gospel makes upon every impartial reader. It is the impression of genuine history. The clearness of the narrative; the accurate references to time and place,— often in apparently insignificant matters, and evidently made unintentionally from the liveliness of the writer's own recollection; the distinct delineation of the different characters,— for instance, of Mary and Martha, of the individual disciples, of Pilate and others, who, though sketched with but few lines, appear so natural and life-like, — all this constantly impresses upon men of the most diverse tendencies, upon such men as Hase and Ewald, who are any thing but uncritical, the conviction,— This is history, and not fiction. Even Schenkel cannot avoid this impression, and sees that he is obliged to refer at least a part of the contents of the Gospel to John. But every division, in whatever way attempted, is arbitrary. The whole Gospel bears one stamp, and its close-locked unity confounds every attempt at division.*

We may now return to the question which we passed over,— the question concerning the relation of the fourth Gospel to the first three. There is certainly a difference between them,— a difference not only in the choice of material, but also in the mode of representation; in the coloring, as it were, of the picture. Difference, however, is not necessarily contradiction. If the life of any remarkable man is full enough to be considered and represented

* See Note VI. p. 157.

by different biographers from different points of view, how much more the infinitely abundant fulness of the life of Jesus!

The more closely we look, the more points of coincidence we find between the Synoptic writers and John. Let us look at the incidents. John relates little concerning the residence of Jesus in Galilee; but he knows that Jesus stayed there repeatedly, for considerable lengths of time. The Synoptic writers tell nothing about an earlier ministry of Jesus in Judæa and Jerusalem; but they know of his saying, "O Jerusalem, Jerusalem! . . . *how often* would I have gathered thy children together, even as a hen gathereth her chickens!"— a saying which seems to imply a more frequent residence in Jerusalem. The Synoptic writers do not narrate the raising of Lazarus; but Luke knows of the two sisters of Bethany, and their character, sketched as it is with but few lines, agrees surprisingly with what John tells of their conduct at the death of their brother. Let us look at the discourses. How many sayings in John call to mind the popular laconic speech of Jesus in the Synoptics! Consider also the saying repeated by Matthew (Matt. xi. 27; compare Luke x. 22), "All things are delivered unto me of my Father; and no man knoweth the Son, but the Father; neither knoweth any man the Father, save the Son, and he to whomsoever the Son will reveal him." Has not this saying, if we may so express it, an entirely Johannine coloring? If it were in John, instead of being in the Synoptics, this very saying would doubtless be used to prove to us that Jesus there speaks differently from here.

We can take another step. The Synoptics and John not only coincide in many ways, — they supplement each other. The fourth Gospel presupposes the three first; presupposes at least the information which they contain. It may be urged that whatever is wanting in John was unknown to him. He does not recount the institution of the Lord's Supper: was he ignorant of that? It is true the Synoptics tell mostly about the Lord's ministry in Galilee: John tells about that in Judæa and Jerusalem. But do these accounts mutually exclude each other? The catastrophe of Jesus' life cannot be understood, on the one side, without a longer ministry in Galilee: on the other side, without a more frequent residence in Jerusalem. It is true the discourses of the Lord in the Synoptics have a different character from those in John. There they are popular, clear and transparent, parabolic, full of telling points: here they are profound, contemplative, mystical and hard to understand; often spoken as if only for a narrow circle. But does one exclude the other? Cannot he who spoke as in the Synoptics, also speak as in John? Was the Lord so one-sided or so poor, that, when circumstances and occasions required it, he could not command a different mode of speech? The Lord's ministry is plainly incomprehensible without both kinds of speech. In John, as well as in the Synoptics, we find the Lord surrounded by great multitudes of people; and nothing is more certain than that he made a deep impression upon the mass of the people. How did he do this? How could he have won those multitudes and bound them to himself if he had only spoken as in John; and not also popularly, as in the Synoptics? On the other hand, whence comes all the fulness of knowledge that lived in the apostolic Church; whence comes the depth of the idea of the divine in Jesus, — if the Lord did not also speak as in John? It is true — not to pass by another difference, which is so much misused — that the Synoptics set forth rather the human element in Jesus: they tell us of the Son of man, the son of David. John, on the other hand, sets forth the divine element more prominently, and shows us the Son of God, the Only-begotten of the Father, full of grace and truth. But it is not true that the divine element is wanting in the Synoptics, or the human element in John. The Son of man in the first three Gospels is also the Son of God, to whom all power is given in heaven and in earth; and the Son of God in John is also a real man, who goes to the wedding, who makes friendly visits at the house in Bethany, who weeps at the grave of Lazarus: indeed, in hardly any other Gospel do we feel the human heart of Jesus beat as we do in John.

In all these ways the Synoptics and John supplement each other; and we say with confidence still more, they require one another. If we had only the first three Gospels, or only the fourth Gospel, in either case we should get only an imperfect idea of the Lord. Consider for a moment: if we possessed only the Gospel of John, we should have no clear view of the life of Jesus. We should have accounts of special, great deeds; but no picture of his daily life and ministry among the people. We should have a sublime portrait of our Lord; but we cannot conceal from our minds the fact, that this portrait lacks distinct outlines. It would not want depth, but it would want clearness. Consider the opposite case: if we possessed only the first three Gospels, we should unquestionably have a very natural, lifelike picture of the Lord. But this would be wanting not only in such external things as several references to time and place; it would be wanting not only in many of the greatest events of his life: it would also want, as Schenkel correctly observes, the unfathomable depth and inaccessible height.* We should have to surmise, instead of beholding, the greatness of Jesus.

Permit me to add to these considerations a word concerning the general relation of the four Gospels to one another. Part of the tactics of our opponents consists in trying to find as many contradictions as they can between the Gospels, and thereby to prove their untrustworthiness. They proceed as if the Gospels were formal legal records concerning the life of Jesus, they subject them to a sort of criminal trial; and every contradiction which they can bring out by cross-examination is made to exhibit the untrustworthiness of one, and consequently, at last,

* Schenkel's Char., S. 25 (Furness's Trans., vol. i. p. 46).

of all four. But they proceed from a totally false idea.

I will try to illustrate my meaning. There is a great difference between a photograph and a painting. A photograph is merely a copy of reality made by a lifeless machine, and therefore in a certain sense it is itself dead. A painting is a living reproduction: the picture has come from the artist; he took it to himself, he worked it out in his own mind, and gave us what he saw. Four photographs of a person must be exactly alike, to the most minute details: if one differs from the others, it is therefore false. But fancy four portraits of a person painted by four different artists: we shall then have four pictures, of which no one agrees with another in every line; of which one brings out one side, another another side, of the person; and still all four are genuine and true likenesses of the same person. Yes: all four together are necessary to make the only complete picture.

I am aware that this illustration is not in all respects perfect: it must suffer the common failing of all illustrations; but I think it will make my meaning clear. The Gospels are not four photographs: if they were, then they who think they can prove their unauthenticity and unhistorical character from every varying line, would be right. They are rather four living reproductions of the image of Jesus. No lifeless machine has given us a copy of Jesus; but living men have told us what they heard and saw of the Word of life. These men differ in their individual characters; and though the Holy Spirit, who influenced them, purified their individuality, he by no means suppressed it. Matthew remained Matthew; and John, John. The image of the Lord was reflected in each one according to his peculiar character; and since no man is able to take and give the whole fulness of the life that is in Jesus Christ, the Providence that rules the Church gave her, not one Gospel, but four; or, to speak more correctly with the ancient Church, One Gospel in a fourfold form.

The Church needed for her life a genuine picture of her Lord. Without it she could have neither arisen nor stood fast. To deny that she had and still has such a picture is simply to deny Christianity. In the apostolic times she possessed such a picture, in the general oral tradition, and in the chosen, personal witnesses who had gone in and out with Jesus. If the Church was to stand, care had to be taken to preserve what she possessed in the apostolic times; and this possession we have in our four Gospels. In the Synoptic Gospels there is the true account of the oral tradition: in them we have what was then told among the people, what the evangelists related on their missionary journeys and on the occasions of religious service in the Church. It is in its simplest form in Mark; in Matthew, the Lord's discourses are especially prominent; while Luke makes the transition from evangelist to historian. His task is to compile, before the oral tradition dies out with the lapse of time. Since the apostolic Church consisted of two great parts, comprising Christians from the Jews, and Christians from the Gentiles; since one who had been a Jew and one who had been a Gentile naturally took different views of Christ, — this difference appears in our Gospels. The Gospel of Matthew represents Christ as he appeared to a Jewish Christian, who saw, above all else in Jesus, the fulfilment of the prophecies of the Old Testament; the Gospel of Luke, on the other side, represents him, according to the reflection of his image in the mind of a Gentile Christian, as the second Adam: so that we may have the likeness of him who should be both the light of the Gentiles and the glory of Israel. To all this is added the fourth Gospel, not a record of tradition, but the work of one man, — of that one of the disciples who leaned on the Lord's breast, who had looked deepest into the deeps of his nature, and therefore was able to present his image as the image of the only-begotten Son of God, whose glory he had beheld.

The possession of the One Gospel in its fourfold form imposes upon the Church the task of knowing the four portraits, which are but one, as one, in order to gain the only full and complete idea of her Lord. Shall I say that this task has been fulfilled? Both no and yes. No: it is a task, in the fulfilment of which the Church has to labor, not in her science alone, but in her whole life, on and on, to know ever more fully the riches of the grace and life that is in Christ Jesus. This task is not to be accomplished by counting the features of his portrait; by a mere book-account of his sayings and doings. This would not be sufficient for the likeness of an ordinary man, least of all for the image of Christ. It is rather a moral task; for they alone can know him who open their hearts to him, and receive his life in themselves: and only in the measure in which his life pours itself into his Church, and takes definite form within her, — only in that measure is the task to be fulfilled.

And yet, Yes. This task is fulfilled daily by every simple Christian soul, who, without learning and science, reads the Gospels in faith, and sees in all four the same original likeness of Him who is its life, and has taken form within it; the genuine historical picture of Him who dwelt and worked among us, — an historical person, and yet exalted above all time; the same yesterday and to-day and for ever.

FOURTH DISCOURSE.

THE MIRACLES.

IN our discussion, a week ago, concerning the trustworthiness of the Gospels, the question of miracles was excepted. We reached the conclusion, that the writings of the New Testament — that is to say, the Gospels — contain trustworthy information about the life of Jesus, by assuming for the moment that the occurrence of miraculous stories in them does not show them to be untrustworthy. We made provisionally the presumption that there were miracles. To-day we have to discuss whether this presumption was correct, — the question of miracles.

We thus approach the burning question of the present, as I have already characterized it at the beginning of my first discourse. Miracles are to so many the great hindrance, the stumbling-block over which they cannot pass! If there were only no miracles, they say, we would accept the rest of the contents of the Bible; but to believe in miracles is no longer possible in the present position of the sciences, — that is to say, the natural sciences. They could more easily give up all faith, than bring themselves to believe in miracles.

This difficulty cannot be avoided. Miracles cannot be got out of the Bible, either by natural explanation or by figurative interpretation. Nor is it of any use to abate something here and there, to set aside this or that miracle entirely, or to conceive its miraculous quality to be less miraculous; for the least miracle is as incomprehensible as the greatest. In vain, also, is the attempt to disjoin the miracles; to separate them as *débris*, and to hold fast only what remains: for all Christianity rests fundamentally upon the miracle of the appearance of Christ; and whoever rejects miracles must also reject the fundamental fact of Christianity, the chief article of the Christian faith. Nor is this all: he must reject all revelation, for revelation is miracle. And if he then, perhaps, comforts himself with the thought that natural religion still remains, this consolation also rests fundamentally upon illusion. To speak plainly, whoever denies miracles has no God. He may always, if only from an instinctive fear of atheism, hold fast that there is a God; but it is a dead word, a name; for this God stands in no living relation to the world. Man has nothing to hope or to fear from him. Prayer is no longer possible; for all praying depends upon the conviction, that God grants what we ask. If God performs no miracles, and can perform none; or, in other words, if he no longer acts in this world, if he is shut out of it, if the order of nature does not admit him, if every thing that takes place is nothing but an unbroken chain of final causes and effects, — then prayer depends upon an illusion; and the illusion must sooner or later become evident to man, shrink as he may from this conclusion of his reason.

I would therefore ask you not to shrink from a clear perception of the whole scope and bearing of this question from the beginning to the end. Strauss is perfectly right in treating the question of miracles as the question of the existence of Christianity. He who does away with miracles not only banishes, as Strauss says, the priests from the Church: he banishes the Church itself, and Christianity, and the living God besides. I do not say this to instil fear into your minds, to hold you fast to the so-called illusion of miracles, through fear of the overthrow of all that we have been used to from childhood. Of what use would that be? It would have no meaning and no blessing for our life. If it is an illusion, then get rid of it, without regard to what falls with it. That would only be doing good, though it should break many an anxious heart. I say it only that you may see what is at stake; and to warn you of the fatal and essentially false ambiguity of those who think that they can sacrifice miracles to the pretended demands of science, without also sacrificing Christianity itself.

Miracles, — what is a miracle? Let us first determine the idea of a miracle; for all that we call miraculous is not miraculous in the sense in which we here speak of miracles. We are accustomed to use the word "miracle" in a very wide sense; and it is therefore necessary to make abstractions from all sides, that we may come to the miracle in the proper sense.

When the seed springs up in the field, and the plant grows from the grain, we call it a miracle. We speak of the miracles of God in nature. It is not to our purpose to inquire how correct this mode of speech is: it is clear that these are not miracles in the proper sense, for they are the effects of mere natural causes. The germination and growth of the seed proceeds from natural forces, according to the inherent laws of nature, without the intervention of a supernatural cause. It makes no difference whether the forces and laws of nature that rule there are known or still unknown to us. When things take place in nature, when effects are produced which cannot be explained by the forces and laws that are known to us, we may say that it is a miracle to us; but it is not a miracle in itself. So soon as farther investigation brings those forces and laws within our knowledge, the miracle ceases to be a miracle. In such cases, therefore, we do not have to deal, properly speaking, with miracles.

It is different with events which are also only the result of natural causes, but in which we must recognize the hand of God, the special guidance and providence of God, because these natural causes exactly coincide to produce just this result and no other. In such cases we can really speak of miracles. Let me give as an example a story from the life of A. H. Franke, the founder of the Orphan Asylum at Halle. One day, during the building of the Asylum, his accountant came to him and asked for a certain sum of money which had to be paid at once. Franke's purse was empty. He went into his chamber and prayed to God; and lo! just as he came out of his chamber, a letter was brought to him containing the required sum. Here we have mere final causes; but in their coincidence with the result, that the money was brought at the very instant the prayer was heard, there is a dispensation of the most special divine providence, an intervention by God, who does not provide the money in a supernatural way, but directs every thing so that the money is at hand the moment Franke's prayer is granted. This is an intervention of God, an actual miracle; but still not a miracle in the strictest sense.

A miracle in the strictest sense exists only when things occur which have their effective cause, not in the forces of earthly nature, but in a direct intervention of divine power, of God himself, (when God acts without the medium of created means.) For instance, when the Lord turns water into wine, multiplies the loaves in the wilderness, raises a man from the dead, — these are miracles in the strictest and most correct sense of the term; and it is with these especially that we now have to deal.

It is necessary to make still another distinction between the miracles of grace which God works in a human heart, and the miracles of power which

THE MIRACLES. 121

take place in nature. Conversion, the regeneration of a man, is also a miracle performed by God; but these miracles of grace, though rightly called by Luther the head and chief of miracles, must, in the first place at least, be left out of our consideration. We shall return to them afterwards; but first of all we have to deal, not with them, but with the so-called miracles of power, or miracles of nature. The question is, whether there are such miracles as the instances already given, events which God himself brings to pass without the concurrence of created, mediate causes.

All the arguments brought against the occurrence of miracles may be reduced to two, — one historical argument; and one philosophical argument, which is based upon the reason. It is said, first, the actual occurrence of miracles is not historically demonstrable; and, second, it is inconceivable, it cannot be reconciled with reason. These arguments mutually support each other; and it is somewhat embarrassing to find out how to take hold of the subject. If we try to prove the miracles historically, it is said, "All miraculous stories are thoroughly untrustworthy, for miracles are inconceivable." If we take the subject by the other end, and, seeking its warrant in the idea, attempt to prove it by reasoning, then it is said, "What does all that avail? Miracles may be conceivable for ever; but their actual occurrence is not established, is not historically proved."

The subject must nevertheless be taken by one

end or the other. Let us begin with the historical proof. This is the most correct way; for, instead of inventing all kinds of conjectures about possibility and impossibility, it is unquestionably better to reason about the facts. This is also the way pointed out by our opponents; for both Renan and Schenkel declare that they do not deny the possibility of miracles, but only their actual occurrence. "It is not, therefore, in the name of this or that philosophy," says Renan, "but in the name of constant experience, that we banish miracle from history. We do not say, 'Miracle is impossible:' we say, 'There has been hitherto no miracle proved.'"* Let us look and see if there is not some instance in which a miracle can be established by sure historical proof.

At the outset we must reject most decidedly the demands which Renan makes for such a proof. He says, "Let a thaumaturgist present himself to-morrow with testimony sufficiently important to merit our attention; let him announce that he is able, I will suppose, to raise the dead: what would be done? A commission, composed of physiologists, physicians, chemists, persons experienced in historical criticism, would be appointed. This commission would choose the corpse, make certain that death was real, designate the hall in which the experiment should be made, and regulate the whole system of precautions necessary to leave no room for doubt. If, under such conditions, the resurrection should

---

* Vie de Jésus, p. xlii. (Wilbour's Trans., p. 44).

be performed, a probability almost equal to certainty would be attained."* Then if the thaumaturgist should repeat the experiment several times upon other dead bodies, under other circumstances, before other persons, we might regard a miracle as proved. — If these demands were just, we should be undeniably and thoroughly beaten; for such a commission of Parisian Academicians never existed in Judæa, and the Lord's miracles also differed somewhat from such experiments made to order before a committee. But the demands are wholly unjust. What would an historian say if he were required to prove in this manner the facts of his history? Strike out the whole history, no fact could be so proved. We regard the miracles, in the first place, as historical facts; and no more can be demanded of us than to prove them, as we prove every other historical fact, by unsuspected witnesses, who can and will tell the truth. Whoever demands more than a simple historical proof, lets it be understood that he occupies the standpoint designated by the saying of Voltaire, that he would not believe a miracle even if it happened in the open market-place, before his eyes; in other words, that, once for all, he absolutely will not believe in miracles.

To prove the historical occurrence of miracles, we cannot now appeal to the Gospels; for we remember that we demonstrated their trustworthiness only upon the presumption that there were miracles, and hence we cannot now prove miracles upon the

* Vie de Jésus, p. xlii. (Wilbour's Trans., p. 44).

presumption of their trustworthiness. This would be arguing in a circle. Let us now start again from the four uncontested Epistles of Paul, in which we have an indisputable historical document.

By these Epistles it is shown to be a fact, that the apostle Paul was convinced that miracles took place at that time in the Church, for he expressly mentions (1 Cor. xii. 9) among the gifts of the Holy Spirit the gift of healing,—of miraculously healing the sick. He was even sure that he himself possessed the gift of miracles. He appeals to it (2 Cor. xii. 12) as a sign of his apostleship. Paul there says, " Truly, the signs of an apostle were wrought among you in all patience, in signs and wonders and mighty deeds." If you say that this conviction of the apostle had no foundation in fact, that he did not really work miracles, you have only this alternative left: you must regard him either as a fanatic, or as an impostor. Indeed, the first part of the alternative is not left you: it could not happen, without supposing a great moral defect. For, mark you, I am speaking of miracles which Paul claims to have performed himself. It is one thing to accept without criticism strange miracles, and another thing to solemnly appeal to one's own miracles. The latter, if the miracles have not really been wrought, is a sign of a great lack of self-examination: it is self-conceit of the worst kind. To believe such a thing of Paul, is psychologically, historically, and morally impossible. I will not speak of the circumstance, that the apostle was not surrounded merely by devoted friends, who in their enthusiasm thought that for him every thing was possible. There in Corinth he had the bitterest enemies; and against these very persons he appealed with perfect composure and the greatest certainty to the miracles which he had performed in their midst. It is easy to say that he deceived himself; but try for a moment to comprehend the character of Paul, as it lies before us so plainly in his Epistles. A man otherwise of the keenest understanding, sober, true, humble; and in this one point weak, deluded, and, what is worse, incredibly presuming and self-conceited. Is that conceivable? Try also for a moment to comprehend his entire work. If you believe that delusion and lying accomplished such great, and not only great,—such blessed things in the world (we ourselves now, after eighteen hundred years, are in the midst of this blessing which the work of Paul extended over our part of the world),—if you believe this, then all I have to say is, that I do not envy you your view of the world, and will waste no more words on the subject. But if you believe, as you perhaps regard the world in other cases, that delusion and lying have a brief triumph now and then, but at last fall under the judgment of the truth, then you must admit that, in this case, there can be no delusion and lying, but truth, historical facts.

It is replied, perhaps, " The declarations of the Apostle Paul are too indefinite: he only alludes to miracles in general; no single one is distinctly named and told. Have you no thoroughly definite miracle that can be historically proved?" I answer confidently, Yes: the greatest of all,— the miracle of the resurrection of Jesus. It is plain, that if we should succeed in proving this to be historically established, all demands would be satisfied. A lively discussion has, therefore, sprung up of late years about this fundamental fact of Christianity. Every power is exerted by one side to destroy it, by the other to defend it.

Let us here also start with a fact which is doubted by neither side, and which cannot be reasonably doubted,— I mean the fact that the disciples, the earliest Christians, believed, and believed with the fullest conviction, that Jesus, the Jesus who had died, rose again bodily from the dead. The whole Church rests upon this belief: this belief is the substance of her preaching; it appears with most complete certainty in all the documents of the time. This indeed does not prove that the fact of the resurrection corresponded to that belief: it is possible that the belief may have existed without the corresponding reality; it may have rested upon delusion. But, at all events, the belief in the resurrection of Jesus is itself a fact, and a fact of the greatest significance for all history, which cannot be passed over without explanation by any one who would thoroughly comprehend the history of our race. Now, whoever refuses to interpret this fact simply in this way, "The disciples believed that Jesus had risen, because he really had risen from the dead," assumes the burden of proving how this belief could have originated and become established without the actual resurrection. The task is even more definite: the belief of the disciples was not a mere indefinite belief, but they believed that they had seen and heard Him who had risen from the dead. This is also a fact which no one can reasonably doubt. We have not only the testimony of the Gospels for it: we have the evidence of the Apostle Paul, who declares (1 Cor. xv.) that Jesus, after he had risen, was seen by Cephas, then by the twelve, then by more than five hundred brethren at once, then by James, afterwards by all the apostles; and at last he adds, that he himself had seen him, referring to the appearance near Damascus.

Let me not be misunderstood. I do not pretend that this belief that they had seen him is all that is needed to prove that they really saw him. I only say it is a fact that they believed that they had seen him, — a fact which must be explained. It is not enough to say, It was an illusion. This is no explanation; for we then ask, How was an illusion possible in this case? And this distinctly states the problem which is to be solved: namely, to show how the disciples could have come to the belief, that they had seen Him who had risen from the dead.

I may perhaps assume that one kind of explanation is exploded, and out of the way: I mean the view that Jesus was only apparently dead, that he recovered from a death-like fainting spell, and that hence the disciples believed that he had risen from the dead. This view of the old rationalism, though it may be found here and there as a relic of past times, no longer needs to be refuted; for, so far as I know, it no longer has a defender. The present prevailing view is, that the belief of the disciples was based upon no objective facts, but merely upon subjective visions, internal sights.

You have all heard, of course, that the occurrence of such visions or hallucinations is a matter of experience. Persons see something, hear voices, without the object which they see and the voice which they hear being really in existence. This is not hard to explain. When the rays of light which proceed from an object outside of us come in contact with the organ of sight, or when sounds meet the organ of hearing, an excitement of the nerves is caused, which is communicated to the brain, and awakes in us the idea representing the object which we see and hear. The excitement is internal; but we learn by experience to think of the object from which the excitement proceeds as being outside of us: we see it outside of us. This same nervous excitement can occur simply internally, without any rays of light or any sounds coming from without, — either from an ill state of health, or from great mental agitation. The same process then takes place: the nervous excitement awakes the idea representing an object or a sound; and, although the occurrence is purely internal, the person thinks, as usual, that the objects are outside of him. He sees an object, a person who is not there; he hears voices which are not there. In this way are to be explained, for instance, the visions of the Maid of Orleans, and the voices which she heard. But we need not go so far for instances of this kind: there are descriptions in the New Testament of undoubted visions, (we may add caused by God; for God uses this means also). When Peter, before the conversion of Cornelius the centurion, saw a sheet descend from heaven, containing clean and unclean animals (Acts x. 9, *et seq.*), the sheet was not really there, — it was a vision.

Such a vision, it is said, was the disciples' sight of Him who had risen, — a purely internal event, to which nothing external corresponded, but which they, as is so common with visionaries, were unable to recognize as merely internal. They saw the risen one, they heard his voice; and were naturally, especially since they were uneducated people, convinced in good faith that he was actually present, and spoke to them. They could not distinguish the vision from an outward event.

At this point we disagree. It is said that they were unable to distinguish between these things: was Paul unable to do it? Paul was able in other cases to distinguish between a vision and real sight. He tells (2 Cor. xii. 1, *et seq.*) of the celebrated vision in which he was caught up into the third heaven; and how distinctly does he describe this occurrence as a vision! On the other hand, whenever he speaks of the appearance of the risen Lord to him, he invariably speaks of it as a simple sight. Besides, the entire context requires this;

for when the Apostle Paul, in order to prove his apostolic worth, appeals to the fact that he too had seen the Lord (1 Cor. ix. 1) as the other apostles had, his sight must have been just such a sight as theirs, — consequently a real, and not a visionary one, — or the reasoning would amount to nothing. When he founds the hope of our resurrection upon the resurrection of Jesus, it is only possible in case he regards the appearance of the risen Lord as a real external event. There can be no doubt upon this point: Paul himself, who in other instances recognizes visionary occurrences, perceives no such thing here. His whole apostolic consciousness, his conversion, his faith, his life and work, are founded upon the conviction that he had seen the Lord, not merely in a vision, but in reality.

Paul was not the only person who saw him. There were also the eleven apostles and the five hundred brethren at once. The fact is established, — it cannot be shaken without arbitrary dealing. Where in the world do you find a vision which more than five hundred persons had at once? How could the same excitement of the senses, the same agitation of the mind, have originated in five hundred persons at the same time? Was it not impossible by natural means? Weisse extricates himself by saying that it was a vision caused by God. In this case I might stop arguing, for here we have a miracle in the strictest sense of the term. Weisse, however, stands almost alone in this view. The aim of others is to do away with the miracle.

Therefore they generally suppose a vision originating in natural causes. But again I repeat, How does it happen that eleven, or so many as five hundred, persons have the same vision? Where is any thing like it to be found?

The greatest difficulty is encountered when one tries to clearly explain in his own mind the origin of this vision, and it is fair to require that this be done. Visions do not arise of themselves: every vision presupposes a corresponding state of mind. The Maid of Orleans saw visions, because she kept herself in an ever-increasing excitement over the ideas which were only embodied in those sights; she heard in the voices only repetitions of her own thoughts. Was it so with the disciples? Did they expect the resurrection? Were they in such an exalted frame of mind, that such apparitions filled their souls? The direct opposite of this is true. If any fact is settled, this is settled, — that the disciples were utterly disheartened after the Lord's death; they did not understand his suffering and dying; a suffering Messiah was totally incomprehensible to them, the cross destroyed all their hopes. Their state of mind at that moment is well denoted by the remark of the disciples on the way to Emmaus: "But we trusted that it had been he which should have redeemed Israel." Is it to be supposed that from this state of mind they experienced the vision; that they suddenly beheld the crucified one as the glorified one? Strauss attempts to make this conceivable. He thinks the impression which

Jesus made on his disciples during his life took a more lively form after his death. They applied the prophecies of the Old Testament to themselves, and found therein that what was said of the eternal life and the glory of the Messiah could only be realized by first coming through death. Besides, they had prototypes in the Old Testament, especially Elias, who also took his body into the heavenly regions. But let me ask, All this change in three days? In three days an entirely new view of the Messiah and his work? In three days an entirely new interpretation of the prophecies? In three days such an entire revolution of all the opinions and hopes in which they had lived from childhood? The *third* day he rose from the dead,— confesses the whole ancient Christian tradition. Even if we grant that such a change were possible without the intervention of some great event, it is too much to expect us to believe it possible within three days. The third day is very troublesome for Strauss; and he devises a conjecture, that the disciples at first, without any idea of a resurrection, returned to Galilee, and that there the change gradually came to pass. But this is flying in the face of history, and substituting groundless conjectures for sure testimony. The third day is not only certified by Paul, and through him by Peter,— we have the most overwhelming evidence for it in the celebration of this third day, Sunday, which reaches back into the apostolic age. Whence comes this unanimous testimony, " the third day he rose from the dead," if on this third day no real event took place upon which the certainty that "the Lord is risen" was based? In the face of this testimony, every possibility of making a vision conceivable vanishes.

There is still another question. What became of the body of Jesus? This question also is very troublesome to our opponents: they try to evade it by every artifice of speech, saying that nothing depends upon it; that now no one can know any thing about it. But let us not be diverted. We repeat, What became of the body of Jesus if he did not rise from the dead? If it remained in the tomb, then tell me why his enemies did not simply point to the tomb, to the dead body lying in it, and thereby put an end to the whole illusion of a resurrection, to all fanaticism and all visions. Can it be supposed that the enemies of Christianity — and it had enemies as determined as they were clever — would not have used this simplest of means to destroy Christianity? Had they no interest in doing so? The announcement of the resurrection was a direct attack upon the supreme council, upon the rulers of the Jews: it contained the gravest charge against them that could be made against a Jew, — the charge that they had killed the Messiah. Yet are they supposed to have kept silence, or to have contented themselves with saying that it was not true, or to have stooped to such weak replies as this, that his disciples had stolen him away; when they could have vindicated themselves at once by the simplest of means, — by opening the tomb and showing the dead body? That is impossible. The tomb must have been empty, as even Renan does not venture to deny. The next question is, Who took the body away from the tomb? I cannot be contented with a number of mutterings about mysteries, and necessary ignorance. There are only three possible answers, — either his enemies, or his friends, or, finally, some unknown third person. Was it his enemies? This is not possible, for they would have said so. Was it his friends? This also is not possible; for then they would have been impostors of the most shameless sort, and I hope that no one here needs to be convinced that they were not such. Then some unknown third person, who, without the disciples' knowledge, for some unknown reason, took away the body of Jesus, and for some unknown reason was silent about it afterwards. If that person had not done it, or had only broken his silence, then the belief in the resurrection would not have arisen. One word from this unknown person, and the belief in the resurrection would have been impossible; Christianity would not have sprung up; the whole course of the world, the entire history of our race, would have been different. Every thing depended upon the chance, that the mysterious Unknown would take a notion, no one knows why, to abstract the body of Jesus from the tomb; every thing depended upon the still stranger chance, that he would keep perfectly silent about it. If you can believe that; if you can make the most significant change in the history of our race, in the whole course of the world, depend upon an accident, — then look to the results of such a view of the world. It would be useless to waste another word against it.

Hume, whose strife against miracles Strauss esteems very highly, tries to do away with them by showing that it is invariably more probable that the best witnesses should have erred, than that a miracle should have occurred. The best testimony is said to have the weight of a feather in comparison with the exceedingly ponderous improbability of a miracle. I think, however, that I have shown on which side the exceedingly ponderous improbability lies. That Paul's whole faith, life, occupation and work were founded upon a delusion; that five hundred persons have a vision at once; that the thoroughly disheartened disciples became totally different persons within three days, without the occurrence of any corresponding event, that the whole course of the history of the world depended upon the chance act of some unknown person, — these, I hope you will say with me, are nothing but exceedingly ponderous improbabilities: and we may venture to say, whoever denies the resurrection to be a fact, deals with mere enigmas and incomprehensibilities. A simple, unbiassed treatment of history compels us to acknowledge the fact; Christ really rose from the dead.*

It is of course always possible to think, in spite of all that has been said, that this cannot be correct. He who cannot explain how Paul became convinced

* See Note I. p. 157.

that he could work miracles, or how the disciples came to the belief that Jesus had risen from the dead, may still assert that no real miracle can have taken place; for miracles are not possible, are not to be reconciled with reason. Then he assumes the point of view from which he does not subordinate his ideas to realities, but sets them above realities; he does not adapt his theories to the facts, but wishes the facts to adapt themselves to his theories; and he is not far from the standpoint of Voltaire,— from saying, I *will* not believe a miracle. Then all discussion ceases. But, from the natural science of the present day, this at least ought to have been learned,— that our reasoning must follow facts, that it is properly only a consideration of facts. This demand alone is just,— that miracles shall be brought within the line of our reasoning, that it shall be shown that they do not contradict a correct reasoning about God and the world.

In the question of miracles, every thing depends upon the view we hold of God and the world, and the relations of God to the world. The atheist, who believes in no God, can of course believe in no miracle. The materialist who knows nothing but matter, finite matter, no Spirit in the world and over the world, can naturally find no miracle. It is equally impossible to conceive of miracles from the pantheistic standpoint. If God and nature are one, the idea of a miracle is self-contradictory; for to say that God does something which cannot take place through the intrinsic powers of the laws of nature, means, from this standpoint, God does something which cannot take place through his own intrinsic laws. As miracles vanish when the distinction between God and the world is entirely removed, so also when God and the world are separated, so that God has no longer any connection with the world, the development of the world runs like a musical clock, which plays the single melody that has been arranged by fixed pins within it. Miracles require a free, personal God, who rules over the world and still works in the world; they presume a relative independence, and at the same time a dependence, of the world upon God.

That is only preliminary. Let us first consider the argument by which some think they can prove the impossibility of miracles directly from the standpoint of natural science. The entire universe, it is said, is an organized whole, with fixed laws. These laws rule not only upon our earth, but everywhere, so far as our observations extend. Our telescopes show that the same law of gravity which regulates the fall of a stone upon the earth, also governs the course of the most distant stars. The spectral analysis has lately furnished the proof, that the same chemical laws prevail in the sun and stars as in the earth. These laws have ruled for ever. The form of the earth, the layers of rocks prove it of a time long before the foot of man trod the earth. Everywhere, wherever we look, we find a close-bound chain of final causes and effects governed by fixed laws. So long as this knowledge of the rule of law in nature was undiscovered by men, they could naïvely imagine that God intervened here and there, that he worked miracles. But since men have discovered this knowledge through the progress of the natural sciences, it is no longer possible to believe a miracle. A miracle on God's part would be arbitrariness; it would be breaking his own law at will: on the part of the world, it would be an interruption of her legitimate course.

It has been thought that the best way of avoiding this conclusion was the utter denial of the existence of natural laws; as is done, for instance, by the ultramontane *Dogmatik* of the Roman-Catholic theologian Perrone. According to Perrone, every thing that occurs is simply the result of a special act of the will of God. The existence of natural laws is only seeming, — they exist only in our thoughts. The fact, for instance, that from barley grows barley, and not thistles, is not the result of a natural law, but in every single case it is the result of an act of the Divine will. The existence also of species and races is only in appearance. There exist in reality only individuals, whom God in every single case guides and governs according to his special will. At the first glance, this view of the world may seem to be the truly religious one. In it there is no more difficulty with miracles. They are works of the Divine will, like every thing else. Every thing is now miraculous; every thing takes place from and by a direct intervention of God. But let us not overlook the other side. Where every thing is miracle, nothing is miracle. The distinction ceases between what is and what is not miraculous. On this account the denial of natural laws is questionable directly from a religious point of view; and it is also questionable on other accounts. It is a mere delusion to fancy that we have any interest in denying the existence of natural laws. Should not the power and wisdom of God appear as great — yes, and greater — to us when we perceive the laws which he has given to the world, by which the stars keep their paths and the worm leads its life in the dust, than when we refer every thing that occurs, in every single case, to a special act of God's will? Indeed, if moral dealing is possible only in a world which moves by fixed laws, have we not, inversely, a moral and religious interest in admitting the existence of laws of nature?

We admit, without hesitation, the premise of that reasoning: the universe is an organized whole, which moves by fixed laws. But does it immediately follow that every miracle, every intervention of the Divine will in this organized whole, is a disturbance? According to the law of gravity, a ball must run down on an inclined plane. If I, by my free will, take hold of it and stop its course, is that a disturbance of the laws of nature? Apart from the intervention of free will, every thing moves by natural law: even the effect which the act of the will has caused remains with its results under the rule of the law of nature. In an uncultivated field, a certain vegetation will develop itself according to the laws of nature, according to the character of the soil, the climate, the region. If man intervenes,— ploughs the land, sows grain, so that a cornfield grows where thorns and thistles were before, where do you find any disturbance of the legitimate course? That which has taken place, however, would not have taken place without the free act of man, which was not done from the necessity of the laws of nature. Why then is it said to be a disturbance, if the free will of God intervenes anywhere? Here also it is true, as Rothe rightly insisted, that the result of this intervention remains entirely subject to the law of nature. The wine which the Lord made at the wedding in Cana was governed by the laws of nature, just as all other wine; the bread which he multiplied in the wilderness, just as all other bread. Is it a disturbance that there is some wine in the world which was not pressed from grapes that grew on the vine; some bread which was not made of flour by a baker? It is no more of a disturbance than that the ball which I hold up does not roll down; than that where man tills the ground a cornfield grows up instead of thorn-bushes. Where is the disturbance in this case?

It is, perhaps, replied, The disturbance is the intervention itself. Very well: the reply only serves to indicate the precise fault of the whole argument. It consists in confounding a system, organized according to fixed laws, with an absolutely closed complex of final causes. That the world is an organized whole, is granted; but that it must be such an absolutely closed complex of final causes, absolutely closed against every other causality, is a proposition plainly unproved, and I may add plainly incapable of proof. It may be shown on the contrary, that, according to reasonable thinking, this complex of final causes must once at least have stood open to a higher causality. A miracle at the beginning must be admitted, unless one is willing to give up all reasoning about the origin of this world.

Let us examine for a moment the train of thought of those who think they can comprehend everything by final causes, and see whether we thereby reach a satisfactory result. We start with the present world, with the present state of animal and vegetable life, and from this go backwards. The perfect, it is said, has developed from the imperfect; the higher animals from the lower. The Darwinian theory shows us, to-day, how all animals are descended from some few original animal forms. We go backwards therefore from species to species, and find, extending up to these original forms, an unbroken chain of final causes and effects. But these first animals, how did they originate? From the plants? Even the natural science of the present day has not made this comprehensible. We stand before a chasm over which we cannot pass without a beginning of creation; that is to say, without a miracle. The animal, as Martensen beautifully says, is a miracle to the plants. But suppose we leap the boundary between the animals and plants, and assume that the first animals sprung, in a perfectly natural way, from the plants; and go still farther back, to the first plant-cells: consequently, to the first mother of all living beings on the earth. But whence did the first plant-cell originate? From inorganic things? At this point natural science says, decidedly, No: never does the organic develop from the inorganic: the living from the dead. We stand again before a chasm, which is still wider than the first; and again nothing can help us over but an act of creation by which the first plant-cell was called into life: hence, a miracle. The plant is a miracle for the stone. But suppose we even pass over this, and on to the time when our entire solar system was still a great ball, a world of cloud; and yet farther, — to the time when the world was still nothing but mere single, separate, freely moving atoms. How did the world, with its magnificence and infinite variety, grow out of these characterless and unrelated atoms? The atoms, it is said, gathered themselves together, nuclei were formed, — but stop; we must let nothing slip: How did this come to pass? I will not ask, Whence came the atoms themselves? I will also overlook the fact, that this whole doctrine of atoms begins to be very doubtful in natural science: I will only ask, How did it come to pass that the first two atoms united? The power that united them cannot have lain in themselves, for they were characterless atoms; but granted that such a power did lie in them, how did it happen that they got in motion, — that this power all at once came into action? Another power must have existed, must have intervened, — a power outside of, above, the atoms, — a higher causality. Whether any one succeeds or not in explaining the whole development of the world from mere final causes, without the intervention of a higher causality, he will never succeed in explaining the beginning, even if it consists simply in the union of two atoms, without such an intervention. As long as this result is not attained, so long may the proposition that this finite world is shut against a higher cause be marked unproved; so long must we lay it down as a demand of the reason itself, that the world is open to this cause; or, in other words, that miracles are possible.*

Possible, — but that is not the same as necessary; and, even if the necessity of a miracle of creation be admitted, that does not prove the necessity of miracles in the midst of the course of the world's development. On the contrary, after God has once created the world, must we not suppose that he made it so good, so perfect, so self-sustained, that it needed no further intervention on his part? It is thus fancied that we gain a religious interest in behalf of the denial of miracles. It is unworthy of God to suppose that the world needs his miraculous intervention, that he must repair it as a workman mends a badly-made machine. We can admit no miracles; because we cannot suppose that the world was imperfectly created.

* See Note II. p. 159.

Certainly not. It was all "very good." But, leaving out altogether the question, whether even a perfectly made world did not require a miracle for its completion (for perfect is not the same as finished), cannot the world *have become* imperfect? Give me an answer from no theory of any kind, but from experience. Thousands of years ago, old Homer said, —

"Of all that breathes, or grovelling creeps on earth,
Most vain is man! calamitous by birth." *

To put a more modern witness by his side, I remember a saying of Goethe's, who was, if ever man was, gifted with all that this world can give. Towards the end of his life he once said, " When I look back over my whole life, and count all the days when I have enjoyed pure, unalloyed happiness, I make up no more than the length of a month." Will you in spite of such avowals, in spite of all the want, poverty, illness, wretchedness, misery and death, still say this world is perfect? For the sake of a theory perhaps you will: what will one not say to save a theory? But experience says, No. If the world is imperfect, — if God cannot have created it imperfect, — then it must have *become* imperfect. By what means? I come to the decisive question, — a question, it is true, rather of the conscience than of the understanding. Is there any sin? Or is that also a childish notion, which we

---

* Odyssey, book xviii. l. 130, 131; (Pope's Translation, book xviii. l. 157, 158).

highly cultivated people of the nineteenth century have outgrown? The Scriptures declare sin to be a fact; and our conscience, whether we like it or not, answers, Yes. A disturbance has thus broken into the world, a hindrance and corruption of its development;* and if the goal of completion which God set before the world shall still be reached, then it needs an intervention of God, a restoration, a miracle of redemption. The fundamental confession of Christendom is, that it confesses this miracle of restoration to have taken place, in that the Son of God became man, and redeemed us. All the other miracles which the Scriptures relate can only be understood in connection with this miracle. The miracles of the Old Testament are premonitions and warnings of this miracle; all the miraculous deeds of Jesus are only single expressions of it. He who came to put away sin, and with it all evil, — sickness also, and death, as the consequences of sin, — heals the sick and raises the dead. He who came to restore the disturbed development exercises power over nature, turns water into wine, and stills the tempest. His miracles are at once prophecies of the consummation, anticipations, prototypes, of what shall take place at the end of days, when the miracle of redemption shall be expressed in the completion of all things, and every thing shall become new.

I may now be permitted to ask again, if that is a disturbance. Do you think it a disturbance of life

* See Note III. p. 162.

10

when a physician restores a sick system to health? I may now ask whether you regard it unworthy of God to thus intervene in the world, healing and saving. It is now very plain how groundless the charge is, that the miracles are arbitrary on the part of God. It is a sheer caricature, and not at all the Biblical idea of miracles, when they are conceived to be incidental interventions in nature at God's pleasure, as arbitrary displays of power, with no other object than to display that power. Certainly they are that also,—displays of the power of the living God, who rules over the world, who gave it the laws by which it lives; and they are likewise intended to show directly before the eyes of men, that there is a living God, who works miracles (Ps. lxxvii. 15). But, in the highest sense, they are manifestations of his love,—miracles of love, of the merciful, redeeming, saving love, which will not let the world that has fallen into sin be lost in it, but will lead the world, that has strayed into false ways, back towards the goal of perfection, which this love has set before it. They are thus the exact opposite of arbitrariness: they are in the highest sense designed.

While looking at the miracles in the light of the divine decree of salvation, regarding them as the acts of God for our redemption, we feel that we ourselves are thus placed in the midst of miracles. The miracle of redemption is constantly expressed among us in miracles, in the sublime spiritual miracles,—the miracles of grace. In the miracles of conversion, of regeneration, of sanctification, we have miracles which do not belong to past times, but which take place to-day; and whoever has experienced any thing of these miracles in his own heart, possesses in himself, in the change of his life, in the peace which he enjoys, in the comfort which refreshes him, in the hope which lifts him up above all else, the actual proof that there are miracles. This proof I can furnish to no one: that must be done by another,— the Spirit, which " beareth witness with our spirit that we are the children of God."

We now return to the thoughts from which we set out several weeks ago. Faith cannot be demonstrated to any one; but obstacles can be removed, and this we ought to attempt. According to my ability, I have attempted it; and if I have succeeded in but a small measure, in proving that our faith is still unsubdued by modern science; if perhaps I have thereby strengthened any one in his faith and protected him from importunate doubts; or if I have been able to rouse any one to meet these questions no longer with indifference, and with the excuse that this has all been done away with long ago, and is worth no more thought,— if I have succeeded in only some part of these things, this is the blessing which I entreat for these discourses.

Permit me a word in conclusion. The present position of the Church is in the highest degree grave. The question is, whether nature shall take the place of the living God — the Lord of heaven and earth — in the faith of our people, and the place of Christianity be assumed by a religion of humanity, if it may be called a religion. It is the question, whether mankind has been deceived by the appearance of Jesus and the spread of Christianity, and has been urged into a wrong road; so that now, since history and criticism, and especially the natural sciences, have shown the Christian faith to be a delusion, nothing remains but to break off its development, and begin again where it departed from the right way, — at the heathenism of the Greeks and Romans. That is essentially the view of a French school, which is represented by such distinguished names as Burnouf, Maury, and others; [*] and Renan is not far from it. This school holds, that, by the progress of Christianity, we have been drawn into Semitic ideas, which run directly contrary to our Japhetic traditions and instincts. The connection with these must be renewed; and then the tendency of the Japhetic spirit, the character of which is described as a pantheistic view of nature, must certainly prevail. Similar views are also expressed among us more and more openly; and some do not hesitate to treat Christianity as a phenomenon whose day has gone by, and which can no longer stand before modern science. The "Life of Jesus" by Strauss is evidently based upon this view.

On the other hand, there are many who think

[*] See Note IV. p. 163.

that Christianity and the Church can only be preserved by squaring itself to the rules of the culture of the present day, from which it is said to be too much estranged. It is said that for this reason we must resolve to give up a part of the ancient faith, to yield some untenable positions to the pressure of science, in order thereby to make more sure of the main substance. From this circle came the "Character of Jesus" by Schenkel. That there are many in this circle who truly and sincerely desire to preserve Christianity and the Church, I do not doubt; but I am none the less sure, that the way they take to do it cannot be the right way. What they abandon is not the unessentials, but the very essence, of Christianity; not temporary forms, but its inalienable substance: and their labor will only serve to prepare the way for those who come after them to reject it altogether. It is certainly the business of the Church to keep in active connection with the development of modern culture; not, however, by retreating before it, but by pervading it with the Christian spirit. To be able to do this, it must neither despise nor shun science and culture. Not every thing, it is true, which is now passed off for science and culture, is true science and genuine culture. No Christian may despise true science, for it is a gift of God; and to do that would be contrary to the declaration of the great apostle of the Gentiles: "All are yours." Nor may Christianity shun any science, — neither history and criticism, nor the natural sciences. It is true that they cannot give us what is highest and best; but we abide in the conviction that they cannot take it away from us, and we are also ready to give an answer to every man that asketh a reason of the hope that is in us. Still the final, thorough, heart-winning proof of the truth of the Christian faith must be set forth by our lives.

I will close by reminding all of you, that the best defence of the life of Jesus is the life of a Christian in whom Jesus lives. Let us all work together in this defence.

NOTES.

ON THE FIRST DISCOURSE.

I AM aware that an authority like Ritter, in his essay, "Ernest Renan on the Natural Sciences and History,"* defends Renan against the charge of pantheism. Pantheism has a somewhat Protean nature; and it is not difficult to give pantheistic thoughts a turn so as to appear as if one only desired, in opposition to an abstract deism, to teach of a God who lives and works in the world. This much, however, can be said with perfect certainty: Renan's God is not the God of the Scriptures. To be sure he says it is an incomplete theology to conceive of God as merely synonymous with "la totale existence," as merely "in fieri." "Dieu est plus que la totale existence, il est en même temps l'absolu. Il est l'ordre où les mathématiques, la métaphysique, la logique sont vraies: il est le lieu de l'idéal, le principe vivant du bien, du beau, et du vrai. Envisagé de la sorte, Dieu est pleinement et sans réserve; il est éternal et immuable, sans progrès ni *devenir*." Let any one compare this with the following sentences: " De qui est donc cette phrase qu'un bienveillant anonyme m'addressait il y a quelques jours: 'Dieu est immanent non-seulement dans l'ensemble de l'univers, mais dans cha-

---

* "Ernst Renan über die Naturwissenschaften und die Geschichte" (Gotha, 1865).

cun des êtres qui le composent. Seulement il ne se connâit pas également dans tous. Il se connâit plus dans la plante que dans le rocher, dans l'animal que dans la plante, dans l'homme que dans l'animal, dans l'homme intelligent que dans l'homme borné, dans l'homme de génie que dans l'homme intelligent, dans Socrate que dans l'homme de génie, dans Bouddha que dans Socrate, dans le Christ que dans Bouddha.' Voila la thèse fondamentale de toute notre théologie. Si c'est bien là qu'a voulu dire Hegel, soyons hégéliens."* The surest criterion by which we may discern pantheism is the question whether the world was created by the God who is supreme above it. Renan recognizes no creation of the world : he at least speaks of none in this treatise, according to the whole purport of which he must have expressed his opinion on the subject. Therefore I think it is doing him no injustice to count him among those who teach what is a kind of pantheism, even if it be rather less palpable.

ON THE THIRD DISCOURSE.

I. p. 92. — The words of Papias, according to Eusebius (Church History, iii. 39), run as follows: "Mark, after he had become Peter's interpreter, wrote out accurately as much as he remembered of the sayings and actions of the Lord. This, however, was not done according to historical order; for he had not heard the Lord, and had not been one of his followers, but had subsequently become a disciple of Peter, who arranged his discourses to supply the wants of the moment, and not as if he had intended to make a regular collection of the Lord's sayings. Mark therefore made

---

* Revue des Deux Mondes, 1863, Livraison 15 Octobre; tome 47. pp. 772, 773.

no mistake when he wrote down what he remembered, for he simply undertook this one thing, neither to omit nor to falsify any thing he had heard." The assertion which is occasionally made to set aside the second Gospel, that this testimony has no reference to it, is groundless. Its importance has lately been more and more acknowledged. Although Holtzmann has made a fresh attempt to distinguish the older form of the Gospel of Mark from the present form, and to attribute only this older Gospel to Mark, yet, according to Holtzmann himself, this distinction between Mark's Gospel and the present second Gospel is so slight, that we must still attribute the main substance of the Gospel to Mark, and hence to the authority of Peter. Besides, Holtzmann has by no means satisfactorily proved the existence of such an original of Mark's Gospel.

II. p. 92. — Papias says concerning the Gospel of Matthew (Eusebius, Church History, iii. 39) : " Matthew put the sayings of the Lord together in the Hebrew tongue, and every one interpreted them as he was able." Irenæus, Origen, and many others, also testify that an original Hebrew writing is the basis of the Greek Gospel. The testimony for the Greek Matthew, however, reaches far back. In a letter which was addressed to Barnabas, and was written, at the latest, in the beginning of the second century, a passage from the Gospel of Matthew is quoted as if from the text. Formerly, since we possessed this part of the letter only in a Latin translation, it might seem doubtful whether this stood at first in the original, or had perhaps been added by the Latin translator. But several years ago, in the old manuscript of the Bible discovered by Tischendorf in the Convent of Sinai, there was found the

Greek original of the letter to Barnabas, and the quotation was found to be the same in this as in the Latin translation.

III. p. 97. — Irenæus, in a letter to Florinus, a friend of his youth, who afterwards apostatized, says, 'While I was yet a boy, I saw thee in company with Polycarp in Asia Minor; for I bear in remembrance what happened then, better than what happens now. What we have heard in childhood grows along with the soul and becomes one with it; so that I can describe the place in which the blessed Polycarp sat and spake, his going in and out, his manner of life, and the shape of his person; the discourses which he delivered to the congregaion, how he told of his intercourse with John and with the rest who had seen the Lord; how he repeated their sayings, and what he had heard from them respecting the Lord, his miracles and his doctrine. *As he had received all from the eye-witnesses of his life, he narrated t in accordance with Scripture.* These things, by virtue of the grace of God imparted to me, I listened to, ever then, with eagerness, and wrote them down, not on paper, but in my heart; and, by the grace of God, I constantly bring them up again fresh before my memory."*

IV. p. 98. — It is worthy of espcial notice, that all the newly discovered authorities of late years favor the Church's view of the Gospels. The oppoite would be expected if this view were erroneous.

V. p. 100. — It has been tought that a strong point

* Neander's Allgem. K. Gesch., Band, iii. Abth. S. 1142. (Torrey's Trans., vol. i. p. 677.)

against the genuineness was found in the conduct of the Church of Asia Minor in the so-called paschal controversy. The Christian paschal supper was joined in general with that of the Jews, who kept their passover on the fifteenth of the month Nisan, after having eaten the paschal lamb on the evening of the fourteenth. But towards the end of the second century a controversy arose between the churches of Rome and Asia Minor concerning the particulars of the observance. The Roman Church celebrated their paschal supper so as to continue their fasting through the week in which the fourteenth of Nisan fell, without regard to what day of the week it happened, until cockcrow on Sunday; and then they began the joyful time of Pentecost with a celebration of the communion. The Church of Asia Minor, on the contrary, fasted only until the evening of the fourteenth of Nisan; then they had a communion service, and went on to the joyful holiday. It made no difference with them whether the fourteenth of Nisan fell on Friday, as in the year of the Lord's death, or on any other week-day. The Church of Asia Minor appeals in behalf of this observance to the apostolic tradition, and especially to John; and this, it is said, is strong evidence against the genuineness of the fourth Gospel. It is said the observance shows that the Church of Asia Minor regarded the fourteenth of Nisan as the date of the institution of the Lord's Supper, for on this day they celebrated the remembrance of its institution by a communion; consequently, they thought the fifteenth of Nisan was the day of Jesus' death. That agrees with the first three Gospels, but not with the fourth; for (this is the further presumption of this argumentation), according to the Synoptic Gospels, Jesus ate the paschal lamb with the Jews on the fourteenth of Nisan, and died on the fifteenth;

according to John he died on the fourteenth, without having eaten the proper paschal lamb. How then, it is asked, can the Church of Asia Minor appeal to John for their custom, when his record of the date of Jesus' death directly contradicts it? The John who celebrated the fourteenth of Nisan with the people of Asia Minor, as the day of the institution of the Lord's Supper, cannot be the author of the fourth Gospel, which says that the Lord died on that very day. In fact, the people of Asia Minor can have known nothing about this Gospel, or they could not have appealed to John.

The correctness of the single presumption upon which this whole argumentation is based, need not be discussed by us. The matter is not finally decided, and the opinions concerning it are very much divided. To examine them now would lead us too far. We will suppose for a moment that such a difference did exist. Now, if the paschal feast of the Church of Asia Minor was as it is claimed to have been, if they observed the fourteenth of Nisan as the day of the institution of the Lord's Supper, we should have a bad case. But this is not correct. Instead of this, the late thorough investigations, especially those of Steitz and Ewald, have shown that the people of Asia Minor kept the fourteenth of Nisan as the day of Jesus' death. They therefore held a communion on that day, in accordance with the idea expressed by Paul and very widely spread in the primitive Church, — that Christ, the real paschal lamb, was sacrificed for us. It was perfectly proper for them to refer to John as a witness in behalf of this custom, and to appeal to the Gospel for it, — by which they meant not the fourth Gospel, but the collective Gospel including the fourth Gospel; for the Church of Asia Minor at least had no misgivings of a difference between this and the first three Gospels.

VI. p. 107. — The attempts to distinguish a genuine substance in the Gospel from later additions and revisions, are based upon the supposition, that the Gospel cannot be wholly unauthentic: they have no other objective basis. There is not the slightest trace of evidence which can be made to favor such a division. These attempts, therefore, are of a wholly subjective sort; and, as usual in such cases, they differ very much, according to the individuals who contrive them. Where one person looks for the genuine substance, another sees the unauthentic additions. Weisse holds mainly that the discourses are genuine; Renan, the historical narrative; Schweizer, in the ingenious efforts which he afterwards gave up, excluded the Galilean miracles especially as unauthentic; while Schenkel finds in the story of the wedding at Cana what is at least a genuine historical recollection. Schenkel has in general followed his own inclination to the greatest extent. He sets out with no principle, but merely with the general supposition, that there is a genuine substance to be traced to Johannine recollections. To actually distinguish this, he does not proceed. A refutation in detail is therefore impossible.

ON THE FOURTH DISCOURSE.

I. p. 135. — Schenkel, in his " General Ecclesiastical Journal "* (vol. for 1865, No. 5), has expressed himself more fully concerning the resurrection of Jesus. He there rejects the view of a natural or miraculous re-awakening of the body of Jesus that had been laid in the grave, and also rejects the view of a mere vision. The resurrection is said to be rather " the real mysterious self-revelation

---

* " Allgemeinen kirchlichen Zeitschrift" (Jahrgang 1865, Heft 5).

of the personality of Christ, which had come forth from death, living and imperishable;" that is to say, the crucified body of Jesus remained in the grave, or was removed in some way now undiscoverable, but he received forthwith a higher corporality, he lived on in a glorified state, and thus manifested himself to his disciples. Since Schenkel himself called this resurrection a miracle, even if not a "miracle of magic, still a miracle of the higher divine order of the world and of nature," I could pass over his view in my discourse, and only remark here as follows: The whole view is contrary not only to the Gospels, but also and especially to 1 Cor. xv., notwithstanding Schenkel's strenuous efforts to appropriate this chapter to himself. Paul assuredly believed that the crucified Christ rose on the third day *from the grave*. This is evident not only from the connection of the burial and the resurrection (1 Cor. xv. 4; compare also what is said about baptism in Rom. vi. 4), not only from the constantly repeated expression, "risen from the dead:" it is evident from the whole argument of the apostle, from the connection of the resurrection of Jesus with our resurrection. Paul teaches not that we shall receive a new, more highly organized corporality, but that our bodies sown in this earth shall *rise from the dead*. An unbiassed exegesis can have no doubt on this point. This view is also beset by the same difficulties concerning the empty grave as the visionary theory. Schenkel will hardly satisfy any one with this view: not those who wish to set aside every thing supernatural, for he asks them to believe something which they will think as incomprehensible as the resurrection; and not those who say with the apostle, "If Christ be not raised, your faith is vain," for they will hardly let this ghost-story be foisted upon them in place of the resurrection. Strauss has made a bitter, but true remark. Schenkel, he said, preserved for Jesus what so many took away from him, — the privilege of ghosting for a while. Violently as Schenkel expresses himself against what he calls the unprincipled dealing of those who mark him as a denier of the resurrection, he has no right to do it. His assertion that he does not deny the resurrection of Jesus rests merely upon the fact, that he has substituted something else for what has hitherto been understood to be the resurrection. Since the times of the apostles, the resurrection of Jesus has been understood to mean that he came alive out of the grave. Schenkel denies this; therefore he denies the resurrection.

II. p. 143. — To show that natural science does not lead away from God, that one can be a great naturalist without losing his faith, I will add a few only of the confessions of great natural philosophers. The epitaph which Copernicus composed for himself is well known: —

> "Not the grace bestowed upon Paul do I pray for;
> Not the mercy by which thou pardonedst Peter:
> That alone which thou grantedst the crucified thief, —
> That alone do I pray for." *

Kepler closes his work on the Harmony of the Worlds with these words: "I thank thee, my Creator and Lord, that thou hast given me this joy in thy creation, this delight in the work of thy hands. I have told men the glory of thy works, so far as my finite spirit could comprehend thine infinity. If I have said any thing unworthy of thee, or

---

* "Nicht die Gnade, die Paulus empfangen, begehr ich,
 Noch die Huld, mit der du dem Petrus verziehn,
 Die nur, die du am Kreuze dem Schächer gewährst hast
 Die nur begehr ich."

have aspired for mine own honor, mercifully forgive me."*
Newton says, "We have Moses, the prophets and apostles,—yes, the word of Jesus himself. If we will not consent with them, we are as inexcusable as the Jews." Ritter, the founder of the modern geographical science, says, "The magnificent structure of the sciences, which man arrogates as his own, and even its highest step, philosophy, is by no means, as he fancies and proudly boasts, only his own creation. It is only the unveiling of the Master's work, and of the everlasting treasure of the truths hidden therein, which, in a partial, earthly covering, the creature is permitted by a special grace from above to perceive and to understand, by the divine light that has been poured into his soul. No branch of science can be a living branch, can be a true branch, unless it springs, free from all merely human devices, from the common root that is deepest of all, and becomes thereby always and chiefly a hymn of praise to God. A thousand branches would spring forth from this tree of life, of eternity, of all knowledge, if the eyes of the spirit were only open, and the zeal of investigation were fired by the aspiration for divine things. The world is everywhere full of the glory of its Creator. Where power and knowledge do not reach, revelation opens the gates to the view of time and eternity." †
Agassiz says, "I confess that this question, as to the nature and foundation of our scientific classifications, appears to me to have the deepest importance,—an importance far greater indeed than is usually attached to it. If it can be proved that man has not invented, but only traced this

---

* Kepleri Op. Om., ed. Dr. Frisch., vol. v., lib. iii. cap. xv., nota viii., pp. 406, 407. Francofurti et Erlangæ. 1864.

† Die Erdkunde von Asien, VIII. Band, I. Abth. p. x. Berlin: G. Reimer. 1846.

systematic arrangement in nature; that these relations and proportions which exist throughout the animal and vegetable world have an intellectual, an ideal connection in the mind of the Creator; that this plan of creation, which so commends itself to our highest wisdom, has not grown out of the necessary action of physical laws, but was the free conception of the Almighty Intellect, matured in his thought before it was manifested in tangible, external forms; if, in short, we can prove premeditation prior to the act of creation, — we have done, once and for ever, with the desolate theory which refers us to the laws of matter as accounting for all the wonders of the universe, and leaves us with no God but the monotonous, unvarying action of physical forces, binding all things to their inevitable destiny. I think our science has now reached that degree of advancement in which we may venture upon such an investigation." . . .

"And though I know those who hold it to be very unscientific to believe that thinking is not something inherent in matter, and that there is an essential difference between inorganic and living and thinking beings, I shall not be prevented by any such pretensions of a false philosophy from expressing my conviction, that, as long as it cannot be shown that matter or physical forces do actually reason, I shall consider any manifestation of thought, as evidence of the existence of a thinking being as the author of such thought; and shall look upon an intelligent and intelligible connection between the facts of nature as direct proof of the existence of a thinking God, as certainly as man exhibits the power of thinking when he recognizes these natural relations."*

* Contributions to the Natural History of the United States of America. By Louis Agassiz. Vol. i. pp. 9-11. Boston: Little, Brown & Co. 1857.

Martius, the botanist, says, "Do you ask me what I have gained as the fruit of a life of fifty years devoted to natural philosophy? Our age is far too much inclined to assume, that the men who devote themselves to the cultivation of the natural sciences are turned away from faith in what lies beyond the perception of the senses, that they give no heed to the warnings of the spiritual basis of things. But who is able, who is obliged, to perceive them more plainly than the natural philosopher, who stands, not at the side of the phenomena, but in the very midst of the stream of life? He certainly knows this, that this great whole was made for only one God; and he also recognizes that something else rules in it besides the laws of the visible world. These he seeks and finds more or less; and his understanding apprehends their harmonious cooperation as the expression of a most high, of a Divine design. But he cannot penetrate to the cause; and, *with the fullest confession of human insufficiency, he becomes humble.* — We trace back the phenomena according to legal series and conditions, but we do not comprehend them in their essence. Far off, in the incommensurable distance, lies their primeval cause; and the θαυμάζειν of Plato, wonder, is not merely the beginning, but likewise the end, of our investigation." When one looks at this list, which might easily be made larger, of the confessions of great naturalists, it sounds strange to hear it constantly reiterated, that it is inconsistent with the present position of the natural sciences to believe any longer in " God, the Father Almighty, Creator of heaven and earth."

III. p. 145.— A few more testimonials from men who will certainly not be suspected of orthodoxy. Schopenhauer says, "If any thing could reconcile me to the Old

Testament, it would be the myth of the fall of man. For in reality the condition of the world looks precisely like the condition of punishment for a great past transgression." "The world is fundamentally only so well arranged as is necessary for its existence. If its arrangement were any worse, it could not exist." Melchior Meyer ("The Controversy concerning Miracles," in the German Museum for 1865, No. 14*) says, "God cannot have created the world in a state of actual perversion." He thinks the men of science have at last become so accustomed to the abomination in the world, that it appears to them to be entirely in order. According to Melchior Meyer the present condition of the world is the result of the fact, that mankind did not stand the test to which they were put, and therefore left the state of innocency. — We see that even they who do not believe in revelation, come through their reason to the fall of man, the result of which is the imperfection of the present world. Let men consider the fact that so much evil and suffering in the world is rather serious!

IV. p. 148. — I cite as an example an opinion of a member of this school, which is quoted in an interesting article in the "Magazine of Foreign Literature" (1865, 14 *et seq.*).† "Weighed down by the custom of eighteen hundred years, careless of our national origin, we are given up to Semitic ideas which diametrically oppose our original traditions and instincts. Nevertheless these Japhetic traditions and the tendency of this spirit are sure of the palm of victory in the future. Preserved and cherished in Greek and Roman antiquity, they were dormant in us

---

* "Der Streit über das Wunder im deutschen Museum, 1865, No. 14."

† "Magazin für die Literatur des Auslandes" (1865, 14 ff.).

for a time, but awoke at the period of the Renaissance, and led us on the path of free inquiry. Profound French thinkers of our day point out our national origin in its authentic monuments; and show that our wisdom is not based upon blind subjection to arbitrary statutes, but that the tendency of this spirit owes its birth and its origin to the careful observation of the great facts of nature that surround us, and of the laws that govern the world. A history which is built upon the foundation of language, a morality and a philosophy which have been won by a more cheerful view of nature, and which, even in their errors, do not deny their source,— the source which springs from the mutual relations of beings to one another, — how highly exalted are they in nobility and grandeur above those dogmas which, despairing utterly of the earth and of mankind, make life a torture-chamber and man a dumb sacrifice." The views of Burnouf, in his work on the Indian Vedas, are similarly developed. According to his view, the original tendency of the Aryan nations is pantheistic; that of the Semitic nations, monotheistic. He also intimates that the Aryan tendency will finally prevail.

www.ingramcontent.com/pod-product-compliance
Lightning Source LLC
Chambersburg PA
CBHW031448160426
43195CB00010BB/895